Letters to my Father

LETTERS TO MY FATHER

Copyright © 2017 by Tammy Jurnett-Lewis

For information contact :

www.iamtammylewis.com/

LETTERS TO MY FATHER

Published & edited by Tammy Jurnett-Lewis

Cover design by P2P Branded

Interior design by IrenePro

ISBN-13: 978-1548096649
ISBN-10: 1548096644

Contents

Foreword - Jon Chaffin..7

Restoration - Tammy Jurnett-Lewis...........................11

It Is Well In Spite of The Pain - Nicole Hampton....................19

Father Daughter Struggles - Tomauro Veasley.......................31

Thank You for Aayla Faye - Jenn Archer................................43

Built by Chism, "Our Struggle"- Angelo Greenhill...................51

Forever a Memory - LeaAnn Fuller.......................................61

Christmas Memories - Nyenye Jordan...................................71

Contents

The Invisible Daughter - Pjai Vegas...................................79

Faithful, Humble, Loving, Kind, God-Fearing, "Richard David Hunt"- Chiquita Ward...,...........85

A Simple Conversation - Tonya Bays.......................,...........95

Dear Daddy - Tammy Pullum....................................101

Questions and Time - Cryss A. Jones............................109

A Testament of Love - Susanna Mason..........................119

While You Have Time - Love Brown.............................149

Foreword

By Jon Chaffin

A father, as defined by Webster's dictionary, is a man who exercises paternal care over other persons; a paternal protector or provider. Key words: Man, Protector, and Provider. I consider myself blessed to have had all three in my father.

I write only from my experiences, as well as my hopes and dreams about fatherhood. I am not yet a father; however, I was blessed to have my father in my life, so I feel that I have a good example from which to work.

I had a great childhood. Growing up, my father coached me in football, taught me how to do a tune up and build a patio. I cut the lawn and took out the trash. We went to Disney World and the Empire State building. He taught me how to tie a tie and disciplined me when I got in trouble. He taught me what it means to be a man; how to make smart decisions and live with the bad ones. We fixed oil leaks and played basketball in the driveway. When I think about the true essence of a father, I think about my dad.

The idea of being a father used to scare me - having to take care of another life. I was trying to figure out how to take care of myself, so, I waited. I made sure that I didn't have kids before I was ready and I'm thankful I did. Most of, if not all of my friends are fathers now. The older I get, the more the idea of fatherhood opens up. It is intriguing to think about having a life to take care of; to protect and someone for which to provide. Having someone who loves you unconditionally.

I don't know what kind of father I will be. My hope is to be the father to my kids, as my father was for my sisters and me. Having my father in my life has had a profound effect on the man I am today, and the father I want to be. I want to take my kids to Disney World, teach them how to swim and ride a bike. Go to their school recitals and cheer from the stands as they play their sport of choice. I want to give my children all the love my parents gave me. I want them to dream big and to believe that all things are possible through Christ. I will read to them, take them to the movies and make forts out of sofa cushions in the living room. I plan to feed their imaginations and encourage their individuality. I want to be a superhero in my children's eyes.

I wish that for every child. I empathize with those who didn't have their father's in their lives. I don't know how I would've turned out had my father not been in my life. But I do believe that I would still be successful, caring and longing to be a great father to my children. There are stories after stories of hugely successful people, who came from single-parent homes, so my belief is that we choose the outcome of our lives. We can choose how we react to life. We can choose to take the pain and turn it into triumph. We can choose to forgive our past and the people in it. We are the makers of our destiny, and though our parents play a major role in our development, it is ultimately up to ourselves to create the life we want.

My father isn't perfect. No father is perfect. However, being there, showing up, protecting and providing for your family--that's as close to perfection any father could get. To my father and ALL the fathers, who are taking care of their family and raising their children, being present and providing a future for them - I Salute You. And to those who didn't have their father, or may have lost their father, my prayer is that you're able to move forward in your life with confidence, courage, and God's Grace.

A native of Stone Mountain, GA., Jon is the youngest of three children. His father, John, is a carpenter and his mother, Phyllis, a fitness trainer. Jon's love for the arts came early, as he would re-enact scenes from his favorite movies and tv shows for family and friends. In high school, he was able to expand his talent, playing lead roles in many of the school plays.

Jon went on to attend Fort Valley State University, where he earned his B.A. in Communications. While at FVSU, Jon developed his talents "behind the camera", producing several shows for the University's Radio and Television station. Additionally, Jon also became a member of Phi Beta Sigma Fraternity, Incorporation.

After graduating, he parlayed his degree and production experience into a budding freelance career, working on numerous television, movie and theater productions throughout the U.S. It was this experience that brought him back to his first love, acting. In 2009, Jon landed a recurring role on the Lifetime series, "Army Wives", playing the savvy club owner, Eric Belton.

Jon would call on his experience at FVSU, when he was cast as Drew, the president of a fraternity, on Tyler Perry's "House of Payne." That same year, Jon was cast opposite Evan Ross and Oscar Nominee, David Oyelowo in the thriller, "96 Minutes." In 2012, Jon worked with Tyler's younger brother, Emmbre Perry, on his film, "No More Games."

His most notable role thus far has come in the form of a crazed gangster, Warlock, on the hit drama series, "The Haves and the Have Nots." Jon has quickly become a fan favorite on the show, now in its 4th season. "The fans love Warlock. I think they relate to his story. That's the joy I get; knowing that it's reaching people and they connect to it."

Some of his other credits include, "Drop Dead Diva", "Charming the Hearts of Men", "Altered", "The Red Road" and "Amelia's Closet." Jon resides in Los Angeles, California.

Restoration

By Tammy Jurnett Lewis

W hen I initially decided to write the book, "Letters to My Father" it was specifically for me to share the feelings from journals that I had collected over my lifetime. Writing has always been an outlet for me. As I began to write and started to remember all the hurt that had been stored from childhood, I decided to expand my platform to others who may have needed the same type of therapy. Because I did so, men and women all over the world have been freed of their past hurts, grudges and pain, including myself. Individuals who never received closure, now have it. Individuals who never had a chance to say good-bye were given that opportunity. For that I am grateful.

After the book was released and I read my story, I could feel the hurt, the pain and anger in my tone as I thumbed through the pages of my childhood journal in book form. Even though writing my chapter was therapeutic and purposed, I realized there were still some unresolved emotions, as I wept through my chapter. I was indeed able to gain closure in some areas, but for some strange reason, I still had questions–questions that would probably never be answered, so I thought.

A short time before I began writing the book, I had been praying for restoration in different areas of my life, not necessarily our relationship, but restoration, in general. Within a few weeks of the book release, my father and I had a phone conversation, unlike one we'd had before. It was definitely an eye-opener, but also a little scary for me. The conversation started out great, became rocky, as we both played the blame game and ended on a fair note with him leaving the door open and ball in my court, and; of course, us agreeing to disagree. As we were able to gain ground and hear the other's concerns, I was overwhelmed with emotions that day, as my father expressed how much he loved me and my children. He explained how he often prayed for us and wanted to have a relationship with the kids and me. He told me things that I had never known–things that directly impacted our relationship. It's funny because these are the words that I always longed to hear as a little girl. I must admit, I've longed to hear them as an adult, as well. I thought that if ever I heard those words that we could just pick up where we left off, but it didn't feel like I could just pick up there, because I didn't know where there was–or if there ever was a place to be picked up.

For as far back as I can remember, I've always wanted my father in my life. He was the one man that I truly loved, but never had access to him. I thought that if I ever had the chance presented to me, I would jump at it. But I didn't. He wanted to meet with the kids and me, but I opted for text messaging. What was it that I was afraid of? Did I not trust him? Was I afraid of finding out that he was not the monster that he'd been made out to be? Or was I just protecting mine and my children's hearts from further disappointed? I don't know the answers to any of those questions. But, I do know that I would, indeed, protect my children at all cost. I am accustomed to pain and I know what rejection feels like, but I would never knowingly subject my children to it--not saying that would have been the case.

As I sat on my bed that night replaying the conversation that I had early that day with my father, I toyed with the idea of going to him, throwing my arms around him and letting him know that I've thought of him almost every day, since I was a child. I wanted him to know the role he'd played in my life, even as an absence father. I wanted to express how I've longed to have a father, and how I've boasted and bragged about him, since I was just a little girl. I wanted him to know how proud I was of him, even if he never felt the same about me. It wasn't long before reality crept back in and I was back in a place of confusion and disbelief.

How much difference would the phone conversation have meant ten years ago? Twenty years ago? Or even forty years ago? I'm not sure. How much different would it have been to know that he had my back and was in my corner? I don't know that either. But the fact that I know now changes my insight about my father. Since that day, we have share a few text messages here and there. I think we both may have reservations. I did; however, feel a little better after having many of my questions answered, and expressing to him how

I've felt all these years. Although I'm sure our relationship will never be anything more than text messages and Christmas cards, for the first time, I am in a good place regarding our relationship. The years that have passed are gone and can never be retrieved. All we can do now is move forward right where we are.

Since that conversation with my dad, I have also reached out to my two sisters. We communicate via phone, text messages and social media on a regular basis now. I feel like my dad freed me up to have a healthy relationship with them. Before our talk, I didn't feel that I could. I know it wasn't their fault, but I didn't know how to let go of the pain of them having the father that I always desired to have. What made them so special? They didn't understand my hurt. They didn't understand my pain. They had both a mom and dad. What did they know about struggling? When I was living out of a car, they were living in homes with swimming pools. Why should I talk to them? Those were my thoughts, and that was how I felt. But as I get to know them, I feel as if the anger I had for my dad caused me to miss out on some great little sisters, not to mention nieces and nephews. I'm glad to have a relationship with them now, and even happier that they have allowed me to be a part of their lives, especially since I treated them so poorly.

I am well on my road to recovery in all areas of my life, and I owe it all to God and writing. I am especially grateful for my first journal. I pray that there are other fathers out there reading these letters, as well as mothers. It is essential that you know how important you are in your child's life. You don't have to live in the home to be a father. I heard a friend say, "Whether a father is in the child's live or not, he still plays a role." That is the outright TRUTH! A real father cannot be kept away from his child, not even by the mother.

Dear Dad,

I am writing a new letter today. The last one, I know, was a little harsh. The words that came across were not meant to be; however, were indeed from the heart. These past few months have been different for me. I don't feel angry anymore, not just because of you, but with life itself. I think you were the last piece of the puzzle. Even though I've done many things, moving past the anger was one I found very hard to master. After our phone conversation something changed on the inside of me. Because I was able to soften my heart towards you, I was also able to soften my heart towards the rest of the world. I can tell that things are different in my life with my other relationships. Prior to speaking with you, I'd been praying for restoration. Again, not necessarily for us, but in all areas of my life. I'm not asking for you to be a father to me, but I would like to someday be friends. Thank you for helping me to bring true closure to that part of my life—the part that continuously hindered my growth. I no longer hold grudges or harbor unforgiveness. Because I've always blamed you for my pain, it would never have dawned on me that you would also be the one to free me of it. So many doors have since been opened unto me, since I made the conscious choice to let go of the past. I look forward to someday hopefully meeting with you again, but if we never have that opportunity, I'm completely grateful for where we are now. I pray that God will continue to bless you, so that you may continue to be a blessing to others.

Tammy

Tammy Jurnett Lewis

Tammy is a Registered Nurse with more than 20 years in the healthcare industry. She ran a successful home care agency called "Ideal Healthcare Services" for 9.5 years, before turning to home care and business consulting. She was recognized in Forbes Magazine in both 2013 and 2014 for the growth of her company and her expertise in the home care industry. She was also recognized in Business Leader Magazine as one of the "Top 50 Entrepreneurs of the Triangle" and "Top 300 Small Businesses of the South." Also, as a recipient of the "Outstanding Healthcare Career Development" award, she continued to work hard to assist in creating jobs.

Tammy has now started an association called "Black Businesses Rock." This association was created to inspired, encourage and assist African American business owners with networking and small business start-up. With her love for writing, she is a Best-Selling Author and is she is now working on her book, "The Faces of BBR" that will showcase several African American businesses from their struggles to their successes. She is best known for her "Camouflage" series. When she is not writing or helping other business owners live out their dreams, Tammy commits to doing speaking engagements at conferences, schools, churches, half-way houses and jail systems, encouraging African American men and women to pursue their life long dreams. She would love to see more of these young men and women turn their hobbies into revenue. Today, Tammy resides in Raleigh, NC where she is happily married to her husband Anthony Lewis. She is also a loving mother of three.

Restoration

It is Well...In Spite of the Pain

By Nicole Hampton

I slammed erratic feet against the bathroom door with enough force for the resulting sound to be heard clearly above the music blasting from the speakers in the living room. With every kick, I released rage, frustration, pain. I hated that man, my stepfather, with every ounce of my being. I hated him for hating me, for stealing my mother, and doing his best to isolate me from her time--her love. Although he effortlessly provided ample reason for me to hate him, I also hated him because he was the poor, worthless substitution I had been provided for a father. However, there was enough hate to share, so I saved some for my real father. He didn't love me enough to come for me, to rescue me from the hell given to me as a life.

Many days as a teenager, I would happen upon my father while walking to work. I assumed he was coming from the grocery store, or maybe just cruising the area since his sister and I lived in the same neighborhood. Sometimes his wife would be with him, others he'd be alone. Each time, he'd slow the car, roll down the window, and try to get my attention. In the fashion of a teen whose feelings of rejection and hurt, manifested as anger and resentment, I would keep my pace, never breaking stride long enough for even a sideways glance. I hated him.

I'm sure the decision to hate the man who donated fifty percent of my DNA was made the night he told my mother, he had other children to take care of, in response to her confronting him for lying about plans to buy me school clothes. I didn't realize it then, but that night marked the first time I felt worthless and unimportant to the man whom I thought was supposed to love me unconditionally. Sadly, it wouldn't be the last.

That night framed my outlook on life and men for years to come. Although, not the sole factor, it was a contributing one to my desire to be an adult. I longed to be able to take care of myself. I wanted to be in a position where I would never have to be dependent upon a man to take care of me. I had learned doing so only led to heart break and catastrophe. I never wanted to get married, so I gave away my virginity as a teen. I wanted to be an adult, and in my world, becoming an adult came with having sex. However, while I was doing adult things, I was unknowingly thinking like a child. I didn't march into mom's house and declare my adulthood, by telling her I had just had 2 minutes of sex with a guy that I imagined would take me away from the misery of life, but not marry. Nope, I kept that tiny bit of information to myself...for decades. I still haven't shared the date that happened, and never will.

20

When I did meet a guy that made me think differently about marriage and spending life with a man, we married. The characteristics he displayed that I fell in love with were those that were present in my grandfather and my Uncle Eugene. He loved me, unconditionally and would do anything for me. However, I didn't trust him to take care of me. I didn't know why he would. I didn't need him to. I've spent most of our marriage being independent, unknowingly demonstrating that I didn't need him. Early on, we both became comfortable with our roles. He did his thing. I did mine. Never thinking to consult one another on matters that affected our family, we lived life together, but separate, comfortably. Little did we know our comfort was silently poisoning our union. When I was ready to change, accept a more interdependent role as a wife, he had not gotten to the same point. The word problem does not even begin to describe what my idea of independence had created in our marriage. It took years for me to realize, my independence was born from a lack of trust that originated from the turbulent re-lations I had with my father.

Over the years, my father and I had many failed attempts at establishing a meaning relationship. During my college years, he would show up and act like he'd been present and accounted for all the time. He demanded a level of respect that I simply was not willing to give. We argued for endless amounts of time, never coming to any reasonable conclusion. He'd drive away mad. I would be left standing with smug satisfaction for having won yet another battle, or so I thought.

When Corey proposed, I did what any happily engaged woman would do, told everyone, including my father. He seemed happy for me, even promised to help pay for the wedding. I believed him. After he made that promise, I visited more often, feeling like he needed to see me in order to remember that he had promised to help. During one of my visits, my brother told me that he needed a new car and our father was going to buy it. I wondered how he would help with the wedding and buy my brother a car. My brother got a car. I had my wedding, without the help promised. He received an invitation, but my mother walked me down the aisle. I still have a photo that captured a look of what I consider anger, at my reducing him to an unacknowledged guest on the most important day of my life.

One year later, I called my father to inform him of the birth of my first child, CJ. I invited him to come and visit, deciding that if he didn't come, I would be done for good. Set on never speaking to him again, elation replaced doubt in my heart when he actually showed up. After Justin was born, Corey and I went to his house to introduce him and my stepmother to their newest grandson. Our relationship improved for a while. We spoke fairly often. Having moved a few times during the course of that seven years, I visited whenever in town. Then Corey moved us to North Carolina and, the relationship changed. This time, it was due to my concluding that I could never have what I always wanted--to be a part of his family.

The first indication of my never being able to gain permanent entrance into my father's family came the Christmas of 2009. Dad called and said, they would not be purchasing Christmas gifts for the grandkids. For a number of years, prior to that time, my kids had gained a coveted spot under their grandfather's Christmas tree. The gifts bought for all of the grandchildren would consume most of the living room. Christmas was a huge deal in my father's house-hold. During those few years, we lived within driving distance, I felt loved by him through my children. He accepted them, in my mind that meant he accepted me; he finally loved me. On Christmas day, my brother posted a picture of all of the gifts our father and his mother had purchased for their grandchildren. Every grandchild had their own mountainous pile, everyone, except my sons. I never told him I knew about the lie he told, but it ate away at my fragile belief in him.

The years since served as time for me to build a case to distance myself once again, and for good. We still talked. I still hoped, but it was never the same. I didn't trust him. When my stepmother died, I didn't get the memo to wear white, and through the obituary, I found out that the man I called father didn't even know my last name. I was listed with my husband using my maiden name. To seal the deal, a few years later, his niece died, and he didn't even tell me, even though he knew I had been keeping in touch with that particular niece's sister, whom I had grown close to, after meeting in 2006 at the only family reunion I ever attended. In my mind, he didn't consider me as a family member.

As I have grown older, more mature and developed a deep, lasting relationship with God, acceptance of my circumstance has become easier. God provided me with everything I needed. I've spent most of my life chasing the love of my earthly father when God has always given it freely. That was something I could not see because I spent all of my years basing the love I have for the man whose DNA I share on contingencies that were impossible for him to satisfy. I also placed contingencies on the relationship I have with my husband. When we had problems, I only considered them resolved if he accomplished certain things, or acted in a certain manner. It wasn't until I learned to forgive, as God forgives, did I finally let go of contingencies. Once I got over being angry and placing effort into mentally distancing myself from my father, I began to realize that we share characteristics. This lead me to believe that such similarities must be innately present because I certainly did not spend enough time with him to emulate his behaviors.   One such characteristic was caring for and loving those who need nurturing. He and his wife adopted two children. He raised three stepchildren and loved their children like they share his DNA. My husband and I are raising one of my sister's kids like we were the ones God chose to create them. Someone else gave them life. God chose us to nurture and protect it.

I have developed a solid relationship with the cousin I met in 2006. We communicate mostly over the phone, calling to check on one another often. Over the years, the love she has shown me has gone a long way in helping me to heal. Having that connection to her has filled a void in my heart, I didn't realize was present. She lived just outside of DC and opened her beautiful, immaculate, kid-free three-bedroom home, to my eight-person family, once when we visited DC for several days. During the day, we toured the famous museums, took hundreds of pictures, and walked until our feet ached with exhaustion. We then sat and watched the droves of diverse human beings traverse across our nation's capital to do only God knows what, after which, we walked some more. As amazing as I found that experience to be, the time with my cousin during the evening, is what will burn in my memory and heart forever. On the first night, she took me on a picture walk through her home, sharing with me the names of the relatives I had never met, whose images were captured in the timeless photos on her walls. Other nights, were spent visiting with other cousins, some I knew from my neighborhood growing up, others I was meeting for the first time. However, the most memorable night was the one she spent telling me about our grandmother, whom I'd only met once, for five minutes, when I was a small child. My cousin described a woman filled with life, determination, and grit. From the story, I gathered that my grandmother played no games with anyone, and was as protective as she was fearless. I finally knew from where I derived a great many of my characteristics. I remember marveling at how much I had in common with a woman; I didn't even know. My cousin has done something in only a few years; my father had never been able to do. She allowed God to use her to weave threads of my heritage into me. She connected me to my family, and indirectly to my father.

The road of forgiveness is long and hard to travel. It is paved with self-righteousness, anger, hurt, despair, self-actualization, and reality. That's just at the beginning. The end is created with love, honesty, grace, mercy, and the open arms of God. However, travel over the beginning is required to get to the end. Forgiveness is the single most important action any person can ever carry out. It is the gateway to many things. Love, joy, and salvation, are some of the most important.

Being able to forgive takes strength and understanding. Sometimes it can take decades to accomplish, but once we get to the point of forgiveness, our hearts are freed from the hurt and pain that had held it captive for an indeterminate amount of time prior. It literally took decades for me to truly forgive my father for what I thought was the greatest mistake of his life... never truly loving me as a father should love a daughter. It took giving my life to God, and not wanting anything to get in the way of the salvation Jesus died on the cross for me to have before I could even consider it. Then I had to dig deep into the hurt that had burrowed into my heart, toss it aside and look for reasons to forgive. When I began this particular journey toward forgiveness, salvation was not enough, although it should have been. I was not, yet mature enough in my relationship with God for it to be enough. However, the one thing that made the greatest difference was the realization that no one is perfect, and we all do things that require forgiveness. I could not reasonably expect to be forgiven for wrongs if I was not willing to forgive.

Understanding that forgiveness was more for me than for my father helped me grow to a point where I could release the pain that had taken up residence in my heart for decades. I had developed a lot as a Christian and was beginning to understand what it meant to be a follower of Christ. Coming to the realization that I had to actually forgive my father, and not simply move beyond my past and him, stopped my growth in Christ dead in its tracks for quite a while. I was literally stuck because I didn't realize my lack of forgiveness toward my father was the root of much of my hurt and pain. I thought it was the issues in my marriage, or being overwhelmed with the responsibility of being a mother of six. I thought it was my being an introvert that made it hard for me to accept people into my heart. I was the type of person that once hurt, I would never allow the one that was the source of my pain to penetrate my precious heart again. Then God began to speak to me and show me what was holding me captive, and keeping me from him. Whenever I would read an article, hear a song, or witness anything that demonstrated the love a father has for his daughter, tears would flow from my eyes involuntarily. For a long time, I would become angry and resentful, but one day, I began to listen to God. I asked him, why my father never loved me. He answered. He showed me, He was enough, and what I was looking for in my earthly father, I could only truly have in Him.

Once that became clear, I lived my life differently, instead of focusing on what I thought I never had, I began to focus on what God had provided, which was all I ever really needed. Every single step in my life has been covered and protected by God, but I couldn't see it because I had not forgiven. Forgiveness did not come easy. I forgave a great many people before I even begin to broach the idea of forgiving my father. I had to first admit that he was important to me. Having spent too many years convincing myself that he wasn't, this was no easy task. In many ways, my actions were childish, a true tit for tat. It was the equivalent of a young child saying, "You don't love me, so I don't love you either." When the truth was I really loved him, and it hurt to believe, he didn't feel the same.

It wasn't until recently that I began to understand how my lack of forgiveness, impeded upon my relationship with God. I could not truly focus on the single most important relationship I'll ever have because I was too busy sulking--too busy looking for impossible contingencies to be satisfied by my father, and those I believed hurt me. I had to let it all go to recognize that I could live in hurt, or die to myself, and live in Christ. In order to truly live in Christ, I had to forgive everyone who had ever hurt me, including my dad, but most importantly--myself.

Yes, I had to forgive myself. All the decades I spent in self-righteous pity kept me from seeing what God had been doing for me all along. When I was able to see it, I acknowledged it but did not embrace it for what it truly was--God's protection, provision, and love over my life. I could tell people about it, but absorbing the full magnitude of it all, evaded the inner most part of me, my heart. I had to forgive myself for all the bad decisions I'd made that could have derailed the course of my life and taken it in a more tragic and sorrowful direction. I had to forgive myself for being angry at a man who did not know how to love me the way I needed. He could not give me, what he didn't have. He didn't have the knowledge of how to nurture a life that lived in a different home. He was not of a world that learned how to express love, through time, and the building of a relationship. I was his first run at fatherhood. At the time, he had no clue what it meant to be a father, and by the time he learned, the damage had already been done.

I found forgiving myself to be the hardest endeavor to conquer. I was so lost. I was a Christian who couldn't figure out my purpose in life because I did not know my own value. It took me realizing that if God could forgive me, and in all of His perfectness, accept me, a sinner, I could let go of all of my self-pity and forgive myself. Stripping away all of the preconceived negative thoughts and feelings took years. I had to face my fears, and face the lack of love I had for myself. I had to get over the idea that I was not worthy of true love. I was only able to do it when I allowed God into not just my life, but my heart. When I came to the end of myself and realized that I had it all wrong, I was finally able to forgive myself. That's when I became free to love God and everyone else more deeply, including and especially me.

Although I occasionally talk to my father, I have not seen him in about five or six years. I don't hate him. I just don't find it necessary to continue to try and gain access to his family. Even without being present, he's had a huge impact on my life. I was determined to show him that I didn't need him. When I was sure he knew, it didn't make me feel any better. The truth is, I did need him. Every daughter needs the first love they receive from a man to be that of her father. It sets the stage for all relationships with the men that come into their lives afterwards. However, God makes provisions for those of us who will never have that experience from the men who helped create us.

Realizing that holding on to resentment and hatred toward my father could keep me out of heaven was sobering. God commands us to love everyone, even those whom we believe have wronged us. He goes as far as to say if we cannot love one another, we can never truly love Him. I can honestly say that I love my father. One day, we may even have a good relationship. However, God is my hope and my provider, all else pales in comparison. Having found true love in Him has allowed me to be free from the past and not be concerned about those who never decided to take up permanent residence in my life. With God in the forefront, I know that no matter what happens with my father and me, It Is Well.

Nicole Hampton's love for reading developed at an early age. She often spent hours becoming lost in the worlds of characters of her favorite books. Born in the south Suburbs of Chicago, IL, reading offered an opportunity for Nicole to dream about life outside of her community and fed her desire to want to explore the world beyond her modest surroundings.

Nicole earned a Master's Degree in Social Work, and utilizes the skills and knowledge learned to address the issues presented in her debut novel Glimmer in the Darkness in a manner that allows people to connect and understand the struggles of her characters.

Nicole lives in North Carolina, is a dedicated wife and mother of six, who spends any time she can snatch, developing characters and story lines to share with her readers. Her second novel, Tears of the Storm, will release in 2017.

Father Daughter Struggles

By Tomauro Veasley, MMFT

"It sucks when the only person who can make you feel better is also the reason why you always cry"
—unknown

G rowing up in a single parent household and being the offspring of teen parents, the odds were already against me. Statistics show 1 in 4 children under 18, total of 17.2 million, are raised without a father. Over the years, I've heard conflicting stories regarding the timeline of my father's presence in my life. Regardless, the facts remain that my childhood is a blur and without pictures, videos or memories it's hard to know the truth. However, I do remember countless nights crying myself to sleep, believing it was my fault, and not understanding why. I spent many years feeling abandoned and unloved by my father.

Why
As the room spins
Round and round
The loud "boom"
Of my tears, break the silence.
I often ask myself why do I cry,
Can someone tell me why?
I mean,
Why do I cry?
No one understands
So, I just ask why...
Why doesn't he love me?
Why doesn't he call?
Why doesn't he want me?
Why doesn't he want to see me?
Why doesn't he care?
She only stares,
But never answer
WHY
When the tears flow
Only Mommie knows
The reason I cry
But the big question still remains
WHY
(Written in 2007)

My childhood memories with my father start in 3rd grade end roughly around 8th grade and then the "darkness" followed. I remember spending a lot of time at my aunt's house with my cousins, because my father was a truck driver, so our time together was spent mostly on the weekends. Those weekends were full of adventures and I enjoyed the time we spent together. Once my father was married, I no longer spent as much time with my cousins and aunt. My stepmother did not have any children of her own, so she spoiled me rotten every summer. Things seemed to be going great.

The summer of 2002, I remember my father picking me up from Detroit, MI in his big 18-wheeler truck and we rode all the way back to Tennessee laughing and joking, when I wasn't sleeping of course. That summer I got a puppy, made a few new friends in the neighborhood and bonded with my new stepmother. My father asked me if I would consider staying in Tennessee for a year just to see if I liked it. I was open and eager to give it a try, but when my mother found out she was furious. By that time, my father had already enrolled me in school and everything. The issues began when my father reacted based off my response but did not communicate and/or get approval from my mother. This small miscommunication spiraled downhill quickly, causing my mother to pick me up from Tennessee. As a result of my mother's actions, within a month or so my father filed for parental custody.

The process was overwhelming, and I decided to isolate myself, because I did not want to choose. I struggled to remain my outgoing, energetic self. This rapid change in behavior landed me in family therapy. The gag-order forbids me to talk to my mother about my feelings and concerns; however, my therapist provided me a safe outlet to vent, cry and process. I was finally starting to feel better about life. I chose to stay with my mother and my request was granted with a strict parenting plan. I continued to visit my father and for a while all seemed well until my world crumbled again. The summer of 2004, I asked my father if I could stay in Colorado for the summer because I had a few dance competitions I did not want to miss. He granted that request. I was happy, and everything was right in the world. Then came Christmas Break and my mother planned to meet my father at the usual location, but he nonchalantly informed me that they had a new baby boy and the family will be out of town. That was the last conversation we had before he disappeared for nine years without any form of contact. For the next 10-12 years I cycled through the 5 stages of grief, experiencing some stages multiple times. The stages include denial, isolation, anger, bargaining, depression and acceptance. The acceptance later encouraged forgiveness. You will identify many of these stages while reading.

In the African American community the role of a father has lost much substance. You often hear people discuss how young boys need their fathers in their lives to teach them how to be a man and how to carry himself. Even more often, young girls are neglected when expressing the importance of a father in a child's life. In actuality fathers shape the course of their daughter's lives because children learn more through the experiences they've lived. Unfortunately, these experiences are not always positive and can have a negative effect on the child's attitude and choices. For the majority of my life, my mother was both the mother and father, in his absence. With that being said, my mother's presence taught me independence, strength and resilience. However, the lack of my father's presence encouraged a lack of trust, lack of forgiveness, how to control and manipulate through sex and helped me draw my conclusion about all or at least most men.

The role of a father includes being your daughter's first love, first hero and the perfect model of what she should marry. Unfortunately, my father and I never had a consistent relationship to get to know each other and for him to provide those necessities. I needed him to model how a man treats his queen and princess, how he supports and provides for his family, how his strength defies all circumstances, how he protects the women in his life against the world, most importantly how I'm supposed to receive and accept love from my husband-to-be. Those are things I wish my father could have taught me.

In 2008, my father broke my heart for the last time, when I received the phone call from my stepmother. She disclosed that they would not be attending my high school graduation. I was an AB student, involved in student government, a phenomenal athlete and I rarely got in any real trouble. In my opinion, I was definitely something special to brag about. My feelings were extremely hurt, and the pain felt like it would never cease. That very moment I vowed to never speak to him again. Not to mention at this point I haven't spoken to my father in 4 years. I felt abandoned and worthless. I could not understand why MY father did not and could not love me. The month of graduation, I decided that I would try another approach to get my father's attention. My plan was fail-proof and he had to oblige because we are both getting what we want. I wanted him to love me and he wanted me to live in Tennessee with him. In my mind, I figured now that I'm grown I can move back to Tennessee and he would not have to go through my mother to see me. This would make it easy for us to pick up where we left off, he would start loving me again and we could have a better relationship. Needless to say, I started undergraduate at Tennessee State University that fall. I quickly found out that my agenda did not merge with my father's agenda.

This harsh reality sent me on a downward spiral and turned my heart cold and reckless. For roughly a year I was in and out of relationships without remorse. As long as things were great, I was happy and content. The first time I felt abandoned or disrespected, I left on the first thing smoking and never looked back. Over Christmas Break, while visiting family, I was sexually assaulted by my cousin's boyfriend at the time. That sent me into an even darker state. Not only doesn't my father love me, but now I think all men are terrible, no good creatures. It was that moment I felt the only way I would feel better was if I got even. I began using sex to control and manipulate the men in my life, such as boyfriends or "friends with benefits". I no longer had love to give. My agenda was clear, I was finally in control and a few even loved me, I just couldn't love them back.

"I'm not mad, I'm hurt... there's a difference"

I finally met a guy that was pretty cool, and I instantly adored him. His name was Wesley. We were together for two years and within that time I learned a lot about myself and what I desire in a man. The first year was pure solace and I enjoyed every bit of it. When I met his parents, it was truly an honor. The way he treated me and carried himself made so much sense. I associated his good manners and genuine spirit with the fact he was raised in a two-parent household. His father accepted me with open arms and to see their interactions alone, warmed my heart. Unfortunately, the relationship ended in another meltdown "dark" place, on my part. I then realized I was still struggling to be the woman I wanted to be, and the father-daughter issues were not getting any better.

Three months after the huge breakup I met a new guy named Bryan. We talked every day and spent every weekend together because we lived in different cities. The vibes between us just felt right, which scared the hell out of me because I'm fresh out of a relationship and I wasn't sure if this was a "rebound" situation. I also had a history of immediately jumping into another relationship without healing. So, I decided to use that year to heal and grow mentally, spiritually and emotionally. I knew and understood that my "darkness" had destroyed the last relationship. Within that year I truly got to know Bryan and I slowly revealed all my baggage to see if he could handle a broken little girl struggling to find her womanhood.

Learning forgiveness was the hardest journey of my life. Bryan knew what the darkness was capable of and, yet he still chose me to be his wife and the mother of his child. I am a firm believer that God places people in your life for a reason. My faults and my past did not scare him away and he allowed me to prove to him and myself that my darkness will no longer control my life. Ironically, he was also raised in a household with two phenomenal parents. Over the years, Bryan and I discussed my past relationship with my father and the relationship I desired. After birthing our son, Bryan encouraged me to reach out to my father more in hopes of a new relationship.

On October 8, 2016 I married my best friend and the father of my handsome son, Brayden. This was one of the greatest days of my life. Every girl dreams of having her father walk her down the aisle in the most beautiful dress of her choice. Ideally, this would have made my day extra special and nothing short of perfect. Well, my father has proven in the past to be unpredictable and I did not know if this dream would become a reality. February 2016, I nonchalantly asked my father if he would walk me down the aisle and provided him with the date and time of ceremony. I can't quite remember his exact response, but it was not a clear and precise yes. My heart was broken for weeks, I cried so much because I was not sure how to interpret his response. In my mind, the response should have simply been, "Of course baby girl, I would not miss it for the world" or "It would be an honor and my pleasure to walk my first born down the aisle." Needless to say, that wasn't it. I began plotting a plan B which included my mother or grandfather walking me down the aisle.

My grandfather only agreed to walk me if my father absolutely declined because he did not want to take that moment from him (I know, my grandfather is an amazing man and I love him dearly). It's now June and I have not heard from my father regarding the wedding. I chose not to bring it up again until around July 2016 and finally he gave me a direct answer. However, as mentioned before, I still wasn't sure if I could trust him to be there. The day before the wedding I texted him and asked if he was still coming and if he wasn't to just let me know now so my day would not be ruined. He promised he would be there no matter what and I smiled. The following morning, he text me saying he was roughly 80 miles away and would see me soon. After the first look with my husband, as I walked towards the front of the church, he stepped from around the corner. My face lit up, I picked that dress up and ran to him. At that very moment my dreams became reality and everything in the past no longer mattered. This was a new beginning and a great start to rebuilding the relationship we both have long desired. Words cannot explain what his presence meant to me on that very day. Not only was he present, he brought my grandmother along with him, LOL, which is another story in itself. I was overjoyed and knew nothing could ruin my beautiful day.

Father's Day 2016 my father, son and husband met for the first time. It was such a breath-taking moment. On that day, I watched as my father's face lit up while playing with his first-born grandchild. As I watched my father and husband bond over conversation and preparing BBQ for the family, I felt in my heart that things were going to be different this time. My father and I also had a conversation about my expectations of him moving forward. He agreed, and we are slowly but surely rebuilding our relationship. On Father's Day 2017, we had a conversation regarding his feelings about the custody battle. I sat in silence and listened to him pour his heart out and express his disappointment. I did not interrupt or comment because I believe it was therapeutic for him to release those feelings in order to move forward without a heavy heart. I whole-heartedly appreciate his efforts and wish things would have played out differently, but I was young and there was a series of misunderstandings. Charge it to my head and not my heart because this too has passed.

Dear Father,

I chose to write this chapter, so you can know and understand how your absence truly affected me. Yes, I was in good hands with my mother, but I needed you on so many occasions. In my opinion, your biggest mistake was giving up and disappearing for 9 years, during the most critical time in my life. There have been a lot of things said and a lot of things done, but I do not want to continue harping on the what, was. We cannot rewrite or change the past, but we can continue to get to know each other and strengthen our relationship. Now that I am grown, with my own family, I do not require as much maintenance. However, there are still a few things I need from you in order to continue moving forward in a positive direction. I need unconditional love and respect, consistency, open and honesty, to be more interactive with us, and most importantly be a dependable and great grandfather. Please remember this jour-ney will be new for both of us, so let's just take it one day at a time. I love you Tyrone Wilson!!

--Forever your daughter

> "The secret of change is to focus all your energy, not on fighting the old, but building the new"
> ~Socrates

Before I end my chapter, I would like to honor my uncle David "Rowdy" Gibson because he was a tremendous father and father figure to those around him. Father's Day 2017, he was called home to be with the Lord. As Brayden said so innocent and sweetly, "he is sleeping with the flowers" and forever watching over us. I love you unk! R.I.P. #ForeverCowboyNation

Tomauro Veasley, MMFT

Tomauro Veasley is from Colorado Springs, CO by way of Maury City, TN. Tomauro currently resides in Nashville, TN with husband, Bryan and handsome son, Brayden. Tomauro graduated from The Tennessee State University with a Bachelor's in Psychology before obtaining a Master's Degree in Marriage and Family Therapy at David Lipscomb University. Tomauro is currently working under Volunteer Behavioral Health Care Systems as an Outpatient Therapist and a School-Based Therapist at several Elementary Schools. She also facilitates a weekly therapeutic group for children and non-offending parents affected by sexual abuse. Tomauro chose Marriage and Family Therapy to become the source of strength, hope and empowerment in individuals, couples and families as they uncover their deepest feelings and innermost thoughts to maximum their potential. As a certified Prepare/Enriched pre-martial facilitator, Tomauro is working due diligently to open private practice. Coming Soon Fall 2018!

Thank You for Aayla Faye

By Jenn Archer

Dear God,

Hello stranger, remember me? Yes, I know I probably do deserve a lecture because it really has been too long since we last spoke. I admit that may be my fault. But if we're being honest, you really do know me better that I know myself so I'm going to assume I'm forgiven...HA HA! A little God humor there for ya.

So how have you been? Busy as usual, I'm sure. What with answering prayers and...well...just being God has GOT to be a lot of work, especially with the whole "No Days Off Policy." That really must be rough. It's like you're a mom or something. HA HA again. Just kidding, but hey you made me this way. I'm just going with it.

Me myself, I'm sure you already know, but it's always a bit difficult for me this time of year and I tend to get sad. Pictures and memories pop up on my Facebook to remind me of what I'm missing out on and honestly it still makes me a little angry. But I do have to admit one thing, even with all the sadness and tears that always go with, I want you to know I am thankful.

I realize there was a time, very recently, that was not the case and I was anything but thankful. Rather I was angry, bitter, depressed, empty, numb, and endlessly sad all day. But who could blame me? You just let my granddaughter die. She was ours and we loved her so very much. We didn't mind that she had Down Syndrome. We were positive and hopeful that the doctors would be able to fix her heart defect and our lives would have revolved around her and everything would have been happy and wonderful. That was our plan. WE HAD A PLAN! I took my daughter, Lauren, to all the thousands of doctor appointments and to the many ultrasounds. We read the books. We read all the books, all the articles and all the pamphlets. We were so prepared. We did everything right, didn't we? And then, before she turned five months old you let her die. In hindsight, it was her mother that eventually had to make the heartbreaking decision after almost a month of watching her get worse, to let her be at peace and have the doctors disconnect the machines that kept her alive. But she was taken from us and that was on You. You gave us Aayla Faye only to take her from us. WHY!

For a long time that was my mind set. Even though I tried to be positive and okay on the outside, reality was I was just functioning on auto pilot. On the inside I was pissed off and so upset with you. I told myself that you and I were THROUGH and I would NEVER speak to you again since it was made very clear you didn't listen anyway!!! What did we do wrong? What happened to prayer works? We Prayed --all the time as a matter of fact. Not only did we pray, but there were people all over the country and beyond that we had never met who were saying prayers for a little baby they had never even met. So, my question is how much prayer does it take because I still firmly believe we met our quota on prayer. Did we not love her enough? I'm confused because just the love I felt alone for Aayla was so intense and fierce that I alone was willing to let her become my entire life. And that was just me. Her Momma, Lauren, had such a special bond of love for that sweet baby girl. There was a connection with that baby so strong I don't think I have the words to even describe the relationship. How was that Not Enough Love?

Again, I was a tad bit upset and said a lot of things I didn't really mean. Just saying...

All day, every day I asked Why? All day every day Dad, still angry--still not talking to you! It seemed to go on forever. Crying at random, at the store, cooking dinner, trying to drive I have no idea how many times I had to pull over to the side of the road because I cried so hard from just thinking about her I couldn't see through my own tears. I always tried to hide it. It seemed better that way, as the rest of my life was still going on around me. I still had to function for my kids and my husband, but it was not going well at all. I stopped caring about things. I started drinking a lot more than I should have, but could care less. I wanted to sleep, all day if possible. It was better than having to feel the horrible ache in my chest from missing Aayla Faye so much. It physically hurt to think about her. I remember there were a few nights I laid in bed with a different kind of prayer-- Not to wake up. It was just too much. And that is what leads me to being thankful.

I'd like to start off by thanking You for continuing to let me wake up every morning even after the nights before when asking you not to do so. I really appreciate that one a lot. Good move on your part.

Then I started to notice other special things that happened due to the existence of Aayla. My daughter Lauren and I met an absolutely wonderful savior to our sanity named Peggy whose daughter, Jackie has Down Syndrome and has become a second family to us. I'm grateful and so thankful for them. And then there were other things I started to notice. They were little things but oh so significant to our recovery. The day Aayla passed we received a call from the hospital saying things were not going well and we needed to come there. We decided to let her go and be at peace that day and finally returned home around 9p.m. that night. When we got home, each of us, including my daughter and husband had a friend to come over and just "Be with Us"-Just to talk or to listen or to watch the Spirited Away movies till 4a.m. in the morning. We didn't really know what to do with ourselves, so I'm thankful for our friends Dustin, Krista, and Analia for getting us through that awful first night. How blessed we were to have friends that devoted and caring. These friends had their own families, jobs to go to the following morning and lives in general to get on with, and they chose to be with us in our time of need. How many people can say they have that? And then it just continued. We had a celebration of life ceremony for Aayla shortly after she passed. I was blown away with the support shown by our family and friends. It was proof that we were surrounded by loving people who genuinely cared about us and willing to do whatever it took to get us through. For that I am so thankful.

Then there were friends who went out of their way to make sure we were doing okay, friends that brought us food and friends that came over just to get us out of the house. We went to flea markets, craft fairs, the movies--just anything to take the focus off being sad. We even had friends that took us camping. It was amazing to see such an outpouring of love. All in all, it was so much more than I had ever expected, and it helped so much with the healing process.

As angry as I was, I was starting to see the good things that were happening due to Aayla's existence. My daughter Lauren had been working a dead end fast food job, but was hired on with the school district working with children with special needs. She is a natural and they love the job she's doing. I'm so proud of her for doing an exceptional job. I'd like to think a lot of that has to do with Aayla Faye and for that I am thankful.

Another perk is my relationship with my husband is so much stronger than ever before because of Aayla. There were no real problems to begin with, but after going through what we did together and managed to survive, in my opinion, is something to brag about. It's given us a reason to love and appreciate each other and our kids even more. We know how lucky we all are to have one another and for his amazing love and support. I am thankful.

Look, I know we ALL must die and the time we get is the time we get. Unfortunately for some, time is limited and seems too short to the ones left behind to grieve. But the fact remains we still get that special gift of time called "Life." No matter how long or short that maybe it still exists and for that I am Most Thankful. Of all the people out here on this big planet that could have been chosen to experience that crazy ride that was Aayla Faye, we were picked to enjoy her. You picked us to love her and it was an absolute honor and privilege. Her spirit and soul were just too grand for her little body to contain here on earth and, so she went home. But for that brief and wonderful bit of time, she was ours and can I just say How Very Thankful I am for that.

Well I've got to be going, but can I just say how nice it was being able to talk to you like this again? I regret it took me so long. But I appreciate that you were so patient and waited for me while I calmed down. I'm sorry for all my anger and I'm really glad you're so forgiving considering some of the choice words I used at times could have gotten me struck by lightning. So, thanks for that too. Be well and keep up the good work. Please hug my grand baby for me, and give her all my love. And again...Thank You.

Love unconditionally,
Jennifer

Jenn Archer resides in Vancouver, WA with her loving husband and 4 amaz-ing children. Jenn is a cook and lives life to its fullest. Jenn's words are, "I have a GED and without a degree. I have led quite the extraordinary life. Just ask Oprah Winfrey, as I was a guest on her show. Here's to living life and being kind. Cheers!"

"Built By Chism, Our Struggle"

By *Angelo Greenhill*

B eing from the country you would think every grandson and grandfather's relationship would be the storybook type--like spending time together and doing things such as hunting, fishing, farming, or just taking the time to learn some type of basic trade. But unfortunately, that was not my situation, not with Howard LC Greenhill also known as "Chism." Chism in today's terms would be defined as a typical street hustler.

My grandfather and I had a very rocky relationship. He was the type of man that literally lived by the quote "Do as I say, not as I do." I had a deep resentment for him most of my life. It almost seemed as if we could never see eye to eye, even when we attempted to be on the same page. From my perspective, I always felt my grandfather was an opportunist and did not care about anyone but himself. The day that I was born, my granddad showed up to the hospital with his entourage drunk and he had a pair of crooked dice. Yeah, I know, but it depends on how you want to look at it. Those crooked dice was the first and only gift I can ever remember my grandfather giving me.

For most of my grandfather's life, all I had ever known him to do for a living was beat people out of their money. My grandparents ran Cafe's on dirt roads in the small towns of rural West Tennessee back in the late 1960's and early 1970's. Chism often boasted about packed houses with Blues and Soul Artists Jackie Wilson, BB King, Aretha Franklin, and Little Milton. My grandfather married my grandmother twice and they had six children together, which consisted of five daughters and one son. Both times ending in divorce and almost getting married a third time before my grandmother backed out.

Chism was an expert with shooting craps, especially when it came to cheating, which got him into a lot of bad situations. He was either going to win it all or lose it all, straight like that. When he was up and winning, he would say things were a little better, but when he was down then the entire family would suffer. I never actually witnessed this, but I recall hearing the stories of how my grandfather would lose all his money gambling, which would result in him going house and becoming physically abusive towards my grandmother, and then he would take her hard-earned money to supply his alcohol and gambling habits. This left my grandmother and her kids with basically nothing to survive while Chism ran the streets and partied until morning.

Chism was a key figure in the club scene back in those days. He ran a club on Pipkin Lane with his friend Otis Hicks better known as the Hill in Madison County, Tennessee from 1967 until

1973--before all his close friends and business partners all died debatable mysterious deaths within those six short years. My grandfather received a message that he was going to be next. The same day his distributor died, a Caucasian male known as John Otis who was also a close friend of the family. So, that very day in 1973 with four kids with my grandmother and a son with another lady, Chism borrowed my pregnant grandmother's first brand new car, that she had just purchased and fled to New York with his girlfriend. He settled in New York in 1973 before relocating to Cleveland Ohio that same year with relatives. Then he eventually moved back down to the South in the later months of 1974. In the words of my grandmother "He came back with a used car and a baby." Chism and my grandmother later remarried in 1975 right before they had their sixth and final child together, which was a boy. That time they stayed togeth-er a little over two years before they separated and later divorced in 1979. My grandmother said that was the best two years they had ever spent together. Chism had changed, got a job, stopped drink-ing, stopped smoking, and was working hard. He was so quiet that you were not able to tell he was in the house. During that time, they also purchased their first home.

Then one day he changed like Dr. Jekyll and Mr. Hyde and went back to his old ways. The old crowd started showing up again, and my grandmother knew he was headed back down that dark road again. One day my grandmother sent the kids outside to feed the hogs and the hogs were gone. My grandmother said at that point, Chism had reached the maximum strikes with her. Her exact words were, "Baseball gives you three strikes out, but you only get two with me." She never told Chism that she did not love him, but the day she left him, she left with God in front of her and with her kids' right beside her. She left the devil behind her and told him do not get too close because he might lose his head.

Even through all of that, I have never once heard my grandmother ever say anything bad about my grandfather. She let us build a relationship and form our own opinions of him. She basically raised all their kids on her own, and never forced him to play his part. From the stories I have heard from time to time, until I got a little older and was able to form my own relationship with my grandfather was priceless. There was never a dull moment with Chism.

In the early 1980's, my grandmother had remarried and honestly I do not think my grandfather ever got over the fact that she married another man. My grandfather had a deep everlasting love for my grandmother, but he just could never find a way to right his wrongs and shake his bad habits. Chism was Chism, and I was told he showed up from time to time to see the kids. A family friend, Peter Miller, used to play the middle man between my grandparents, by picking up the younger kids and taking them to see my grandfather.

I think in the early 80's my grandfather was dealing with a lot of untreated depression and he handled his problems by hitting the bottle. He had lost all of his closest friends in the 70's to unexpected deaths, and he lost his mother in the early 80's. Chism was crazy about his mother and in his eyes, she never thought he did any wrong. He was a momma's boy. He was staying with her at the time of her death, and was the one to discover her body on the morning that she passed away from a massive heart attack. I never heard him say much about his father. All I knew was his father was a lot older than his mother, and my grandfather resembled his dad. He was a tall soft-spoken fair skinned mulatto man with pretty coal black hair. He spent a lot of his last years as blind years. My grandfather had eight brothers and sisters and they were share croppers in the earlier years of his life. He talked about how they worked hard all season getting out the crop and the farmers would cheat his dad out of the money. I think that was the start to my grandfather's ambition to chase money. One thing I can say about my granddad is that you could not tell him "no". He thought that anything and everything was possible, and he was going to find a way to make it happen.

I was born in 1984, and I rarely recall seeing my grandfather throughout the 80's. I remember the occasional "hey boy" and pats on the head when we did run into him from time to time. He was kind of like a drifter, a myth and urban legend. One thing I can say about grandfather is he was well respected in the streets. Chism literally had nine lives. One particular incident I recall hearing about was an altercation my grandfather had with a man and he was shot in the mouth. The new paper article read "Man Shot in the Mouth and Swallowed the Bullet." I know right, and that was just one incident. Chism had his throat cut, a woman tried to burn him alive, numerous car accidents, and the list of myths goes on and on. I heard these stories all the time, but it was not until the 1990's when I actually began to build a person relationship with my grandfather.

He started to come around a little more and would babysit my cousins and me, on occasion. I had not made it to my teenage years yet and there was a lot I did not understand. My granddad had a bar-b-que standoff on Gasden Highway in Fruitvale Tennessee. He was arrested in 1994 for a host of charges, including crack cocaine possession with the intent to sale. Even though that was not his first time doing time in jail, that was the first time he was incarcerated, and it affected his grandchildren.

The first time I ever visited anyone in jail was my grandfather.

I can still remember the entire experience. Back then in Justin Crockett County jail, all of the inmates in the facility were housed together. The trustees had the ability to move around a little more freely, but the rest of the population was a little scarier. It was literally one huge cage with a bunch of individual cells, and there were four beds to each cell. Imagine how I felt as a kid visiting that place and seeing the worst of the worst criminals cramped in a small area the size of a gymnasium. All the inmates looked mad and miserable, and the visitation process was even worse. We actually went to the area where all the inmates were and the only thing that separated the inmates was a yellow line and a row of rusty iron bars. As we walked in, I remember my cousins and me holding each other's coat tails at the same time trying to hide our fear. Keep in mind that in the streets the myth of my grandfather was like a guy whom was larger than life. We rarely saw him, so I really did not know what to expect from him. Then this older soft-spoken man walked up to the bars and said "Hey." At that moment for the first time, I felt like I met the real Howard Greenhill instead of Chism. The visit was brief, but one thing grandfather said to us that day that has stuck with my whole life. He said, "Look at these niggaz. You do not want to come in here, do you?" We all shook are heads no and then he smiled and walked away. After he served a few months, Chism got out of jail and finally relocated back to Alamo, Tennessee, where he was close to the rest of his family. From that point on, I saw my granddad on a regular basis.

I grew up in Nashville, Tennessee, but I spent all my summers in Alamo, Tennessee with my grandparents. Chism was what I call a wide-open hustler. His house kept a lot of traffic because he bootlegged whisky and sold his share of crack cocaine. In those times, we were getting a little older and curious. Even though we were raised to do the right things, I somehow took after my grandfather. I consider myself to be a very observant person, in other words, I may not have said a word, but I watched everything and did not miss anything. In my teen years, I was introduced to marijuana, and started to sell it a little bit as well. The crazy thing is I had good parents and came from a good home, but fell in love with making fast money. I was able to make pretty good money when I was in high school. I remember lying to my mom about how I was getting money on a regular basis.

Looking back now, I can admit that I was lost. I was struggling in school, and with my life in general. I graduated high school in 2003 and moved out of my mom's house the following day after my graduation. I moved to Alamo, Tennessee lost and with money on my mind. I was familiar with dealing crack, but never really sold it myself. I used my graduation money, and that $100.00 changed my life forever. I remember sneaking and stealing my granddad's sales for almost one year before he even realized what I was doing. He told my grandmother all the time, "Them boys selling that stuff, and that Gigalo is sneaky." As always when my grandmother confronted me about what he said, I would deny it, and that is when mine and my grandfather's conflict began. For years, I believed my grandfather was jealous of the relationship I had with my grandmother. At the same time, my thoughts were that he should be practicing what he preached.

He had been back in our lives for a while and it seemed as if everyone had a personal bond with him except for me. Mine and my grandfather's relationship came from the fame. He was totally against me hustling unless I was making runs for him. I felt as if when he wanted to short somebody, he would send me to make the run for him. I would go to keep down any confusion, but I cannot remember one time that he sent me somewhere and the package was actually right. Once I started refusing to go, then things got worse between us. For a long time, I thought he hated me. Truth be told, I was so ignorant at that time, I honestly did not care. Chism was drinking heavy and was into church more. He had stop drinking and started going in and out of jail for more offenses, mostly driving while his licenses were suspended. Although seeing him drunk was the funniest thing you could ever witness. He would become angry, and if he felt it, he would say it. We did not make the situation any better because all we did was to gas him up to act more foolish. Between 2005 and 2006, I started to notice a change in my grandfather. He slacked up on the hustling, and for the first time in my life, I saw this man work a job. At that time, the new and present Crockett County jail was being built, and he was hired to be a part of the construction crew. Shortly after the jail was completed, he was hired to work as a part of the cleanup crew for a local factory.

Meanwhile, I was all over the place. I was young, paid and felt like I could not be touched. I was one mistake from spending a lot of time in the penitentiary. I did a whole lot of things I am not proud of, and some of my actions resulted in a lot of people getting hurt--Some of which were close to me, as well as people that were not. Threw all of that, I managed to maintain and keep a good job. At that time, I was really living two lives. I learned early on how to turn it on, and turn it off when need be. I was finally able to see why my grandfather and I clashed so much. I realized I was him all over again. Everything that I resented and hated about my grandfather was the same thing he hated and resented in himself, and I was the spitting image of it. I reminded him of all the stupid things he used to do. My grandfather had already changed, and was leading a better example. I gradually started to follow his lead. When we lived together, we rarely talked unless it was about money. I relocated to Jackson, Tennessee and started having kids of my own. I began looking at life differently. I slowly started cutting ties with my circle. My grandfather and I stated to talk a lot more about life, mistakes he had made, God, and most of all his relationship with my grandmother. He shared with me that he wished he would have done things differently. At that time, I was young, and he was very fond of my girlfriend whom eventually became my wife. He would ask me how we were doing. I was not in the streets as much, but I was not the perfect boyfriend either. I still had my flaws. He would ask me questions like "Do you think you guys are going to make it?" He also said, "That girl is good for you because she does not take your crap." Then he would drop his head and give that little grin. Every morning my girlfriend would at the time drop me off at my grandmother's house before work, because my job was in walking distance from her house, and we had the same routine. My granddad would hop in the car with her, and she would take him to get coffee. When she dropped him back off, we would talk for about fifteen minutes before I went to work.

One of the last conversations I remember having with my granddad was him saying "Boy I use to worry about you all the time, because you were always into something. It would have hurt me if something would have happened to one of us." He then told me that he loved me, and that my cousins and I kept him going. On that day, I shed a tear walking to work. That was the first time I had ever heard my grandfather tell me he loved me. Little did I know that my grandfather had been fighting cancer for a little over two years. During that time, he was able to repair his relationships with all of his kids, including his step-daughter, whom he loved and cherished. To me, my grandfather was a living proof of the statement "it is not how you start the race, it is how you finish it." He always said that family is everything, and if one of us have something then we all have it. My grandparents taught me the biggest lesson of my life, which was, if my grandmother could forgive my grandfather for all his flaws, then I should be able to forgive anyone for anything they have done to me. My grandfather passed away November 1, 2008, and my grandmother took care of him all the way until his last breath. I was standing right beside her, with his bed surrounded by seven of his kids.

Angelo Greenhill is a TN native, currently residing in Memphis, although originally from Alamo, TN and raised in Nashville, TN. He is married with five beautiful children. Angelo is the CEO of Living and Growing Apparel also the president of Knocdown Worldwide. Founders of the Knocdown-SCM awards.

Forever
A Memory

By *LeaAnn Fuller*

Dear Dad,

I found your birthday card the other day. I couldn't believe I still had it nearly 25 years later. It was also hard to believe that some days could still be hard, and I could still miss you so much.

Most people have probably never thought much about the half-time of that game on December 1, 1993. The memories faded just like the paint on the walls. The walls have been painted since then, but my memory of that horrible night never will. I often wondered if you knew what was going to happen that night, or if you suspected that something was wrong. I figured you must have known something was wrong just before it happened, because you sent Kerri out to get some candy. You never let her get anything, especially at half-time, because it was too crazy in the foyer.

I remember you dropped me off that night before the game. It was the first varsity basketball game of the season. I was only a JV cheerleader, but we were there for the halftime routine. It didn't matter to you because you came to everything. You were our biggest fan and somehow, we all thought we were your favorite.

You and Kerri were taking the movies back to Oriskany Falls and planned to return be before the game. I am sure I was probably late, because I spent hours in the bathroom doing my hair, man that drove you nuts. That was the last time we spoke, as I jumped out of the town highway department pickup truck. I really wished I could remember what we said, but I don't. I guess that was the downside of being a stupid teenager-- we took those small moments for granted, and we never paid attention, until those moments were gone, and we wished we had.

I don't remember much about the game or the halftime routine. I do however, remember seeing you sitting up there in the stands, as you always were when we were done and were headed out for half-time. Little did I know that would be the last time I saw you.

We always headed down to the 2nd classroom just past the foyer to take our break and get snacks and drinks. There was always lots of laughs and giggles, while we talked about how horrible our routine was, or maybe wasn't, or how someone's hair or outfit looked.

But that night, it was disrupted with a lot of ruckus and yelling out in the hallway. Being curious, okay nosey, we had to check things out. Apparently, someone had fallen in the stands and they called 911 from the maintenance office across the hall from where we were. That was of course, before the times of cell phones. I remember Lyle came down and I overheard him telling them someone had fallen and was unconscious and hung up, then hurried back to the gym. He walked faster than normal but it wasn't until he came back, nearly panicked that time around to call the ambulance again that we really paid attention. They realized the gentleman hadn't fallen, but collapsed from a heart attack and they needed the ambulance there faster. Granted it was a small town and there was always an emergency, but there was a difference in the urgency of someone falling and someone having a heart attack, especially when it was one of their own.

I really didn't think too much of it when he looked at me and closed the door. But, why would I? I just figured it was for privacy, or we were loud or something. It wasn't until it was time to head back to the gym and we were in the foyer that I noticed something strange was going on. Everyone was looking at me and acting odd. That was when I saw one of my neighbors, that was a couple of years older than me, holding my little sister just outside of the gym doors as she cried that it really set in as to what was really happening.

It was at that moment I realized it was you that collapsed in the stands with a heart attack. I remember hearing you guys so much of it from that very instant really became a blur. I vaguely remember that I cried hysterically and collapsed. I remember Carla, our neighbor came over to me with Kerri and grabbed hold of me too.

I remember I asked for you. All I wanted was to see you, but they wouldn't let me. They said they were taking you to the hospital. I wasn't sure if you were okay or not. The only reason I had even known the seriousness of what was going on was from when I heard you guys talking after your surgery. They said if you had another heart attack, it would most likely be your last.

Mom and everyone else had gone to Syracuse. So, there I sat holding onto Kerri in a bundle of tears. Lost, confused, and helpless surrounded by people that wanted to help, but really had no idea what to say or do. I really didn't know what to do with myself, or worse with Kerri. At the time, I knew she must have been scared, but she was too young to really know the magnitude of the situation.

I remember she went home with some friends and another had taken me home. I laid in your bed curled up in a ball, cried hysterically, and asked God why. It was then that Grandpa came in and said he wished it were him. My reply was, "So do I." I know that he was trying to make me feel better while he tried to reach mom to let her know. At that moment, I couldn't imagine why God would take you from us and leave someone like him with us.

It seemed like forever when some friends showed up to take me to the hospital. All I could think about was getting to the hospital to see you, because I still had no idea if you were okay or not. So, I jumped at the chance to get a ride to the hospital, and I had no idea when anyone else would make it home. I didn't realize they were going to drive around forever. I wasn't sure if that was their way of making sure mom got back in town, and got to the hospital before me. I really didn't know, but I was so angry that they didn't just take me to the hospital, that I couldn't cry anymore. What must have been hours and hours later, we finally arrived at the hospital. I think I was the last one there to find that you were in a coma on the Intensive Care Unit. Even to this day, I still remember when I turned the corner of the hallway towards the ICU wing and saw most of my family there, as they hugged and cried. My tears began all over.

They were still evaluating things and really weren't sure the extent of the damage at the time. But I finally got to see you. As I walked into the ICU, it was so dark and dreary, and I was so overcome by the scent that it took me back a bit. I walked into the room and saw you on all those machines, the constant beeping of the machines, the gasping sound of the ventilator breathing for you, tubes and wires coming from everywhere. I could hardly tell it was you any-more. Your hands and arms were so rough, cold, and clammy to the touch. I begged you to wake up.

The next nine days nearly blended together and were some of the hardest days of my life. Mom and I never left the hospital. Well I did, once when Shawn showed up. It was hard for me as I really couldn't understand where he was coming from, but it wasn't until years later I realized how hard it was for him as well. Carl convinced me to take a break and to get something to eat with him, so we went to Burger King. As hard as it was to leave, it was nice to get out of there for even a few minutes. I knew he had the best of intentions, but it was so hard for me. I really didn't know what to say or how to let him in to help.

I think the worst part of it all was realizing that there really was no hope of any return for you. Overhearing the conversation with mom and the doctor where the decision had to be made to pull the plug was devastating for me. After days of testing and waiting, they had determined there was no brain activity. You had always told us that you NEVER wanted to live life like that. We knew that we had to follow your wishes no matter how hard they were.

We came to terms with it, and found comfort, or at least we tried to, after the fact that you lived over eight years on 20% usage of your heart. Dr. Cohen said that it was nearly impossible. But considering the love you gave from 20% of your heart was probably more than anyone with a normal heart, it almost made sense.

December 6th mom made what must have been one of the

hardest decisions of her life-- to take you off from life support. I know saying goodbye to you and watching you take your last breath was the hardest moment in my life. At my age, it wasn't something you ever expected to do. We expected that our parents would live forever, especially when you were one of the best people in the world.

You took your very last breath, and left the place with a bang, literally. As you left, the ceiling collapsed in the room next to you, thankfully no one was in there. I wasn't sure if that was your way of taking the sting out of it by getting us to talk about something else, to keep us from crying anymore, or just to give us one hell of a story and left your lasting impression on the place as you always did. Whatever the reasoning, you were successful. Between the collapsed ceiling, the broken taillight that got us pulled over on the way home from the hospital, the broken dishwasher, and everything else that seemed to go kaput shortly after. We joked that you apparently wanted to take it with ya. We still do.

Mom and Wendy really pushed to get through the services as quickly as possible. The last thing they wanted was to have your funeral on my birthday, for which I was thankful. It was hard enough having your funeral the day before my birthday. It was a hard pill to swallow, since I was turning 15. Mom tried so hard to salvage my birthday though, for which I love her dearly. I'm not gonna lie, all I really wanted to do was lay in my bed and cry, but they dragged me out of the house, and we all went for a family dinner, regardless of how hard it was for all of us. I still struggle from December 1st to the 9th every year. But every year come the 10th, I pick myself back up to celebrate my birthday, it's like starting the new year fresh. I think it is the way mom handled it back then that has allowed me to do so. I know that couldn't have been easy for her.

Your calling hours were hard even though the tears were gone.

Once you spend so many days crying, there isn't much left. I only cried twice, when Shawn and a few friends from school came. I'm not sure why, other than I was just so grateful to have them there, especially as withdrawn as I had been.

Life became extremely difficult after we lost you. I was lost. The next year of my life was a total blur. I don't remember if I even went back to cheering that year to be honest. I think they offered me a pass from gym for the remainder of the year. I don't remember if I took it-- I sincerely don't remember much. I pushed everyone away from me that cared, and I started to head down what could have led to a very dangerous path. The next thing I knew I was pregnant-- 16 and Pregnant! It was a huge wake up call. But apparently one I needed.

I wish I could say that I snapped right out of it, but I didn't. It took me a while to wake up and realize that things just weren't right. You know, it took me years of being yelled at and treated poorly to realize that I didn't ever recall a time of you and mom fighting. It was you and mom that taught me what a real relationship was supposed to look like. It may have taken me a long time to wake up to it, but I did. I remember Lee telling me that all I was looking for was my dad, and I was never gonna find him. Boy, am I glad he was wrong.

For that I am so thankful to you. I am so thankful for the amazing man that you were. I am so thankful that you showed me who a man is supposed to be, and how I should be treated. It took me such a long time to figure it all out and listen, but I did.

I do sometimes wonder if I let you down through it all. I know it took me a while, but I figured it all out. I'd like to think that you are looking down on me, and are quite proud of who I have become. I think I am a lot like you. I know everyone jokes that I must be the milkman's kid because of my red hair, but I do think I am too much like you to not be yours. Every time I talk to someone and my kids ask me who someone is, I remember tugging on your pant-leg and asking," Who is that dad", often with a shrug and just making conversation.

I always look back so endearing at what an amazing man and an amazing dad you truly were--back to the days of you singing, "Hey good looking. Whatcha got cooking" and riding on the tractor with you, or into you when Kristen let me drive the first time. Helping you out in the garden, and planting your rows and rows of glads. You letting me put barrettes in your hair. Nights at DeRuyter while you found someone to chat with, while we were having fun. You showing up after us in the wee hours of the night (Your plan for keeping Kristen under wraps didn't always work out to well). Your brake checks when you were checking the roads to see if you needed to send the plows out. Your Christmas light contests with your friend from work. Last minute Christmas shopping at the old store, and going next door for some hot cocoa. I never liked waiting for you to get done plowing to open presents at Christmas, but it was always the best when you got home.

I could go on for days with stories and my favorite memories. I love to share with the girls, and all your grandkids. It's one of my favorite things to do when we are all together, sharing memories of you and mom. I miss those days, and I miss you so much every day.

If heaven wasn't so far away, I would pack up the kids for a day.

I love you.
LeaAnn

LeaAnn Fuller is a successful Entrepreneur, Women's Transformational and Fuller Life Coach, Amazon #1 International Best-Selling Author, Motivational Speaker, and Radio Show Host. She is the founder and CEO of Fuller Life, LLC where she empowers women to get out of their own way to transform their life, find their greatness, and to live their Fuller Life. She empowers them to find clarity about what it is they want, why, and what is standing in their way so that they can quit living small and begin living their Fuller Life. She is also the founder of Adopt-A-Mom for Christmas to give back to moms in need over the holidays that she is turning into a year-round movement to support single and struggling moms year-round. She is the Program Director for WBOC, The Premier Organization for Women in Business in CNY.

Website http://welcomtoyourfullerlife.com/
Facebook https://www.facebook.com/FullerLifeLLC/
Twitter https://twitter.com/FullerLifeCoach
Radio show www.blogtalkradio.com/sagenetwork

Christmas Memories

By *Nyenye Jordan*

Dear Dad, or Poparoni,

I want to thank you for all of the Christmas joy that you added; I should say created for us. Even through all the chaos and noise in our lives, you made Christmas, and every holiday special. All past discretions were forgiven and forgotten. All disagreements and heated exchanges were laid to the side. None of those things was a factor when it came to our happiness and enjoyment at Christmas time. It gave me a since of normalcy that even through the trials we were normal people.

The first thing that comes to mind is you and mom up all night cooking. After I was married, the plans changed to you all coming to our home and spending the night, so you could be with the grandchildren. You supervised like you were the master chef. One Christmas you even barbequed, in the frigid Michigan weather, with snow on the ground, because you wanted ribs for Christmas. You would make pound cakes. They were the BEST! I remember you got the recipe from an egg carton. For the life of me, I cannot remember which brand of eggs; I really want that recipe back. But those are just a few of the moments that make Christmas so special, even now. I remember your diligence, your "we will make it happen" attitude. Nothing was too good for your kids. We truly felt special. Not arrogant, but set aside, like we had a special place in your heart. I know that we did, and you have one in my heart. You're good outweighed the bad in our lives. I think we put you on a pedestal, in our minds we had the smartest, strongest dad around. Christmas simply sealed the deal, let us know you were the greatest.

One of the first Christmases I remember, I don't know how old we were, we had to be young. We found out where you and mom had hidden our gifts. Now you never taught us to believe in Santa Claus, and I truly thank you for that. We were allowed to go out and pick our gifts, except for one or two gifts that you hid from us. Those were our surprise gifts; we knew about them but not where they were. The anticipation each year grew. We couldn't wait for those surprises. Well, one year we didn't wait. We snooped all around the house looking for those gifts. I must honestly say that even though he was the youngest, Kamau was the ring leader. He convinced me to help him look for those gifts. I knew better but the suspense was killing me as well. But I didn't think they were in the house. I just knew you had taken them over to Aunt Shirley's or Aunt Wavie's house. Our quest started every time you and mom left the house for a moment or were out of sight long enough for us to do a quick sweep of the area. We eventually we hit the jackpot. On the right side of the walk-in closet in your room were big bags filled with our surprise gifts! We spent the next few minutes, it felt like hours, ohhh-ing and awwww-ing over the items in those bags. We must have heard one of you coming so we put things back as quickly as we could. We climbed out of the closet and acted as if all was well. We underestimated your sharp memory and attention to details. I don't remember if it was later that day or a few days later but you reminded us just how sharp you really were. You called us into the room as if you knew nothing of what we had done. You picked our brains for information until we cracked. We admitted that we had indeed been in the closet and were fully aware of the gifts that had been hidden in there. I was trembling at those words. I just knew that we were going to get the whipping of our lives, and although my brother was a trooper when it came to whippings, I on the other hand was a wimp. Just the thought of getting a whipping made me cry. But after our confessions you stood there smiling and began to laugh. You said, "They are your gifts, you just won't have any surprises on Christmas. That was it, no whipping, no scolding, just laughter. You always amazed me like that. The things that I thought would take you over the edge never did. You understood our curiosity. I think you were proud to be able to give us the types of gifts that you probably never had as a child. The greatest part was we still had surprise gifts on Christmas morning! The trick was on us. We truly enjoyed that Christmas. Thank You Poparoni.

Christmas was not always about gifts either. It was more about family time. Us being in the same house with each other. Us sharing food, fun, and fellowship. Us talking, up until the wee hours of the morning, often times falling asleep on the couches and waking up to resume conversations and fun. You, dad, gave us that. You made it important to us. Even now we talk about what you would say and do during those times. It brings a tear to our hearts but a smile to our faces. I am so very grateful that my children got a chance to experience you and all your glory. It seems to me that you were the best gift, and memories of you are our forever reward. You taught the kids so much during our visits. All my children learned how to tie their shoes by the age of 5 because of you. Now we have a two-year-old, who is going to teach her to tie her shoes? (I guess she will always wear Velcro shoes, lol).

Tears come to my eyes as I write this letter. You were and are so much to me. I know now that I took you and your presence for granted too often. So many other children had so much less from their fathers, and I had a jewel in you. As our life situation changed, I focused so much on the bad characteristics that I may have missed out on some of the good that you possessed. You were an anomaly, an oxymoron, my Poparoni. I miss you. During each pause as I wipe tears, I remember another way that you touched my life; there are so many. Words truly cannot express my love and adoration for you. I pray that you knew how much I adored you and your knowledge. You were a genius! If I had half of your knowledge, I would be a millionaire by now. Christmases just give a small glimpse of who you were and how big your heart was. Isn't it crazy that it was your heart that took you away from us? Just at a time when I think we had both matured enough to have long, meaningful conversations. At a time when I could share with you my deepest secrets, aspirations, and goals. I know that you would help me run the nonprofit, edit each book, go to each of the boy's games, love on Jasmine, spend time with mom, enjoy the family reunion, see your brother as a free, changed man and so many other things. Your life and our relationship have truly provided a platform for me to reach my goals and live out loud. Thank You.

Now the Christmas that I remember the most was when I was around 14 years old. It was unseasonably warm in Michigan that year. There was no snow on the ground. Most of us were glad even though we secretly wished for a white Christmas. But the snow could vanish after Christmas day. I woke up, along with my brother expecting a lavish spread of gifts under the tree. Well, to our surprise there was nothing. You informed us that you had a night of gambling, either cards or the track and we had nothing. Surprisingly we weren't upset. All I had wanted was a pair of riding boots. They were all the craze that year along with stirrup pants. You instructed us to get dressed. Mom continued cooking our dinner, which we enjoyed later that day. We got dressed, and you took us over to Canada. We had been there before visiting granddaddy at the Windsor Raceway. I really liked that racetrack. They had good hot dogs and was a bit fancier that Hazel Park. I assumed that was where we were going, to see your dad and maybe borrow some money. Boy, was I surprised when we went shopping. I guess because Christmas wasn't celebrated on the 25th of December in Canada, their malls were open. We went to some type of outlet mall. It was great. The people were so nice and waved. We shopped until we dropped. I got those fancy riding books and a bunch of stirrup pants to go with them. We had a ball. We talked, laughed, and saw the trees and what looked like the countryside. It was breathtaking. We came home with gifts but more importantly was we came home with memories. You didn't let us down. The next year brought its own difficulties but that year prepared us for them, mentally and emotionally. Thank You

Dad, Thank you. Thank you for the memories. Thank you for the good as well as the bad times. I don't know if I would even call them bad times at this point. Yes, there were some rough patches, but they were also learning experiences. Yes, there was some pain associated with them, but there was also laughter, assurance, confidence builders, and affection. I wouldn't trade those times for the world. The lesson has been invaluable. You have given me the ability to write finally-- my life dream. I could never do it while you were here for fear of hurting your feelings, but now I know that some things you knew all along. You recognized that you had flaws and there were times when you could have and should have done better. But you also realized that I had developed a relationship with both you and our Father, God. You knew that relationship would supersede all others, including ours. You knew that once I put my trust in God, He would heal the pain, wipe all the tears and use the bad to create greatness in me. You knew it would all work together for my good. Wow, you were more than just knowledgeable, you were wise. You knew that God had placed others in my life who took up all the 'slack" when you weren't at your best. You allowed those people to pour into me, and you continued to pour into others. You planted seeds that not only nurtured you but provided for us as your chil-dren. I see the picture clearly now. When I was a child, I thought and reacted as a child. I am a woman now, and I see through our relationship clearly. It was perfect for us. I have found that I can indeed be content in every situation. I am not only content with our situation but overjoyed that things have come full circle. So once again, Thank You, Dad. You will always be my Poparoni, my genius, my go-to guy, the first man I ever loved unconditionally. I have tried to put my feelings into words for you, but they still come up short in expressing my true love and respect for you and the life you lived. My prayer is that you see the goodness of you in me, and when the bad does arise because I am my daddy's child, that our heavenly Father tames that spirit in me. Thank You, Thank You, Thank You.......

Love, your favorite daughter

Hello, my name is Nyenye Jordan. I am a mother, wife, survivor, nurse, min-ister, and servant of God. I am a dreamer and at the age of 41, I decided it was possible to turn my dreams into a reality. So now I can add author and entrepreneur to my list. I thank God that He has kept my mind throughout each storm in my life and He has given me beauty for ashes. I encourage ev-eryone to put your trust in God. He is a rewarder of those that diligently seek Him. I thank God for my husband, my parents, and my children. All of them have brought such joy, peace and priceless memories to my life. I thank God for all the powerful women that he has put in my life. They have encouraged me to live beyond my wildest dreams! I am truly blessed beyond measure. I pray that something within the pages of not only my story but each of the stories offer you hope, peace and assurance that everything will work together for your good. Be Blessed.

Nyenye Jordan

www.nyenyej.com
Nyenye.jordan@yahoo.com

The Invisible Daughter

By **Pjai Vegas**

"It would be too easy to say that I feel invisible. Instead, I feel painfully visible, and entirely ignored."
–David Levithan

Dear _____,

Being the first of your two daughters, one would assume I had a special place in your mind. Being the first of any of your children, one would think you'd like to be there for all my firsts; ups and downs. One would be foolish to assume such thing--I know I was. I have learned your caring to be imaginary and untrue though I have never been able to understand why. I often wonder how many times in 23 years I crossed your mind.

My memories from childhood were not pleasant enough to re-member vividly, at least not when it came to you. I remember your mother's house (Not at any particular age or year), and I remember your childhood room where I'd sit on a water bed and watch TV for hours. I remember vaguely, times I spent in that house with my sister or alone--but one thing I don't remember is you. In fact, the only memory I can recall is being at Chuck E. Cheese's and taking a picture in the photo booth. It was the only photo I ever took with you, and I have never forgiven myself for losing it. I don't imagine my sister ever had that problem.

With each year I got older, I started to notice things that were different between my sister and me. I gathered from stories that she had a family. When her mother married, I remember thinking she could have three parents to love her, while I didn't fully feel loved by the only one who cared about me. When she became a big sister, I realized how much I felt jealous that she had a sibling, and a family in her home. She seemed to have everything and the one thing we were supposed to share, I was deprived, because of your choice. To this day I've always wondered why you hated me so much, compared to her. I mean, we are thirty days apart in age--so was that all I got? 30 days to be important? What about me made it okay in your eyes to walk away and never look back?

For years I tried to channel the rage and hate I felt, but even as a strong 'Jesus Freak' teenager, I never really found a way to forgive you. I'd sooner forgive friends who stabbed me in back, since at least at one time they actually cared about me. Driving by your mother's house after church would always entice strange feelings in me, but I went a long time not thinking about you or my sister. Not out of spite, but out of distraction. I had found other things that deserved my tears, and I felt that I had been set in where we all were. My sister wasn't really my sister, because I didn't know her, and you weren't my father since that seemed to be what you wanted. However, the feelings never stayed buried too long. Once the hurt diminished, something would happen to bring all my rage to the surface. It is anger that overflows so much, I still think about changing my last name, so I can cut the little connection we have completely. But as strange as it is to say, the anger is not what keeps me hurting. It is the tears. Tears that I am sick of crying over you, a person who doesn't deserve my tears.

Even being held back by anger and sadness, I tried to connect with you. I tried to help you care about what was going on with me. I invited you to my graduation and ceremony to send me off to California. It took everything in me to put myself out there and hope, even an ounce that you would show up. I honestly would not have known what to do if you had shown up. But I didn't have to worry because you managed not to attend either event. Though I wonder if you could imagine how I felt to see photos of you celebrating with my sister, as she graduated soon after. There you were, glowing with pride for your daughter.

It was worse than a slap in the face.

I thought just for a moment you had changed when your mother passed, only a short year after I moved here to California. You called me out of the blue to tell me, and in the same breath, you managed to choke up an apology for never being there for me. But the silence for the next three years showed me that you weren't too sad about missing out on my life, either that, or you don't understand that things must change in order to be okay. I truly think it is the latter. The year after my grandmother's passing, I was invited to have dinner for your birthday, while I was home visiting. I don't think it was you who invited me, and I don't recall why I agreed to go. I was stuck there with strangers who were supposed to be my aunt, uncle, and cousin, wedged between a girl I'd vaguely known to be my sister and you. The only thing I remember from that night was your comment; "I've got two daughters to take care of me." Even today, four years after the fact, I want to laugh and scream in your face about it, but I see now that you don't understand what was wrong with it. You have never understood that for twenty-three years, well twenty at that time. I've never felt like your daughter. In fact, you had never understood that. I knew nothing about anyone on your side of the family. As far as I had seen, your family saw you as having one daughter.

You could never guess the hate I felt towards everyone, except my grandmother. The annoyance I would have for an Aunt who has known nothing about me and makes empty apologies for neglecting me. Or hate for my sister who has never done anything to wrong me. She had the love and presence of you that I couldn't understand why I couldn't get, even though I tried. I wondered if you ever thought about the fact that your children were not bonded in any way other than half of their DNA. It hurts me so much that she is a stranger, but that is my fault. Ever since I was a child, the only thing that made this whole thing easier to deal with was disconnection. At one point, I had to accept that I would never be a part of your family. Over the years it became easier to see a picture and say, "This is my biological father and his daughter." Even with her soon to be married, I am preparing myself to see photos of you walking your princess down the aisle. I don't intend to sound bitter; this is just how I have learned to be.

Now please understand that I do not write this letter to tell you that you are terrible, or to tell you that you should feel ashamed. This is the first time I have been able to lay out how I have felt for 23 years. I wish I could write everything I have ever felt, but that would be a book of its own. I have prayed to be able to forgive you, but even now, it seems like it will never happen. The problem now is that I am an adult, so I can initiate movement in our relationship, but why would I bother. I've tried before, and the non-existent effort on your part made me feel more unloved. I don't want to have to feel that any more severely than I already do. I don't mean to sound hateful or angry in this letter. I don't want you to feel sorry for yourself. I want you just to see me. That is all I have ever wanted--for you to try to understand that your invisible daughter has been here the whole time, hurting and never understanding why she was (and still is) purposely ignored.

Don't take these words and pain as signs that I have had a terrible life without you. I have had a good life and, every day I try to make it even more amazing. I hope you can understand that I would never feel the things I have felt if I didn't have a love for you in my heart. If I have ever said that I hated you, it was out of anger for feeling like there was never any love for me in your heart. I will still pray to forgive you one day, but it will not be easy. So, if you ever do reach out, please be aware that I will be hesitant, and I may want to shut down. But if you are willing to try, then so am I.

Jalyn Robinson is a native Texan currently residing in Los Angeles, California under the name P.jai Vegas. After receiving a degree in Vocal Performance, she began work as a vocal in-structor for children and adults. She is currently studying to branch out to international music genres, performing at a variety of Korean Events since 2015. Her hope is to travel to various countries to collaborate with musicians and producers and to work with organizations fighting for causes near to her heart.

Faithful, Humble, Loving, Kind, God-Fearing, Compassionate— "Richard David Hunt"

By *Chitquita Ward*

Dear Daddy,

I miss you so much. I have never known so much pain as the day when God called you home. As a Christian woman, I know that one day we all will go home to be with our Lord and Savior, but I was truly not ready. I feel that God was preparing me as I reflect on things now. As I look back at the time he gave me with you, especially the last year of your life, 2011. How ironic was it that I was laid off the exact same year you passed away? God gave us that time. God gave me those memories to cherish. God made a way and put people in our paths to allow us to travel together, enjoy life together with mom and your grandchildren because He was coming for you sooner than we could have imagined.

Chiquita Ward

I don't know if you knew this or not, but you were my everything. Losing you, I felt as though I lost myself. All I've ever wanted to do was be successful, but it mattered to me that I made you proud.

I think back to when I was a child and some of the special things we did together. I remember waking up on Saturday mornings with it being you and me because momma was asleep. I remember you putting my hair in a puff ball, throwing clothes on me and hitting the road. You started a Saturday ministry of feeding the homeless and serving the less fortunate. I remember going with you and thought it was awesome. I felt a sense of pride as I helped serve food. I was happy to be helping someone else. Afterwards, while the choir was rehearsing, we peeked our heads in to listen to some good Traditional Gospel Music. If you had a meeting, I'd sit with the choir, sometimes singing. I remember our time singing so much. My first solo was "Goin' Up Yonder." As I got older, we sang duets. The one we sang most was "I Love Jesus More Today." I loved the moments when you called me up during service to join you in a song. That was "Our Thing, " and I miss it so much. I miss singing in church, but I miss singing in church with you most.

When I started high school, I remember you always being there to support my being in various activities, but what remembered most was marching band. Because the band did lots of traveling, you were there to drop me off and late nights to pick me up. Even though I loved it, as I got older my interests changed, and I wanted to quit and do other things, but you didn't allow me to quit. You felt that it was important that I finished what I started. For that reason, I stuck with it.

All my friends enjoyed hanging out with my parents.

They thought you guys were cool, strict, but cool. We had our Hermitage Crew, and we were as thick as thieves. People felt as had nothing to do with the other. There were just somethings I could NOT do; if I wanted to go to a party, you would take me, and you'd be there to pick me up. The same thing stood if I wanted to go to a friend's house, you took me and was there to pick me up. If any foolishness were to take place, it had better get wrapped up before your arrival.

I remember the first day of college. You and mom dropped me off at Middle Tennessee State University. I was scared to death. Although I had many friends that were also attending, I was not 100% ready to leave the nest. College was a lot of fun, and I enjoyed my newfound freedom, but everyone knew who you were. If you were not showing your face on campus, I was bringing friends home with me on the weekends. I enjoyed bringing friends home on the weekends and having them go to your church on Sundays. I loved for them to hear you preach and sing. Not only that, we had an amazing time at home with you and momma. Once I had a dream that you died in a car accident. I was a nervous wreck. I called repeatedly, and you didn't answer. I was certain it wasn't a dream. About an hour later you called me and said, "I'm outside. Let's go to lunch." It was things like that-- you being there when I needed you most that resonated. Time passed quickly. It wasn't long before I graduated. You were so proud. I was proud and accomplished, but most of all I was your daughter, a young, educated black woman! I remember you telling me that I had the world at my fingertips and all I had to do was to put my mind to it and trust God and I could do anything I wanted.

As a young woman, I remember the biblical advice you gave me about dating. You were there through all the ups and downs. Dating was a hoot! On my wedding day, we had the best time. You were clean, FYE, my daddy, and father of the bride. We laughed, clowned, cried, hugged, cracked jokes as we always did and shared some priceless moments, all captured by the photographer. You held me close, walked me down the aisle and gave your baby girl away to my then husband. You and mom made my wedding day so memorable. It was like a fantasy wedding. It was elegant, glamorous, exciting and more than I could have ever imagined it to be. Thank you for that daddy!

The example that you set as a parent was amazing. You set the bar high. The example that you set for a husband was even higher. You were the example of what a man should be. You were the epitome of a humble, God-fearing man who lived by what he preached. You, daddy, were a hard act to follow.

I wanted and desired to be and wife and mother. You and mom were married 40 years, and it was beautiful. I wanted EXACTLY what you shared. I wanted a love like that. I wanted something genuine and pure. I wanted a love that God put together. When a man loves God, he knows how to love his wife. That is what I wanted. You worked so hard to take care of momma and me. I can't remember ever asking for anything that you didn't get for me. I never wanted for anything growing up. You always took care of business. I can laugh now, but I was broken-hearted then; I stayed married long enough to have the most beautiful children in the world. When my first child was born, we were so happy. You were so excited about being a grandfather. You spoiled me rotten, took care of me and was the perfect daddy. I remember when you and mom rushed me to the hospital after my water broke. You were tickled, and I was anxious, but when that baby boy made his arrival into this world, you were so proud to have a grandson. You were the same way at the birth of my second child. You were there, and it was the funniest thing—I had her on a Sunday, and you had to go to church and preach. You first came in to check on me, kissed me on the forehead and told me you'd return after moving the car. By the time you returned, your granddaughter had made her grand appearance in the world. You were the best grandfather ever! I thank God for the time He allowed you to spend with my children. They will never forget you. As long as there is breath in me, I will keep you in the forefronts of their minds, as you were very inspirational in raising them. We often talk about the quality time you spent with them. They remember you taking them to school and picking them up, as well as the daily trips to McDonald's. It's your fault that they love pancakes as much as they do. They re-member the slip and slide in the yard and you running to pull them down the slide. My timing was perfect for having kids. You were retired and had a chance to spend all your time with them. They remember the trip to Disney World and how much fun it was. I have so many pictures of us from our last family vacation–pictures of you playing with them in the sand and taking them in the water at the beach. We rode the roller coaster rides. You and mom were champs and rode with us. I will never forget that vacation. God put people in place for us to take that vacation. All we had to worry about was food for the week. God gave us that special time.

My heart gets heavy when I fast forward to 2009, and you received a diagnosis of Cancer. I was so angry. I just couldn't understand how that could happen to you. I couldn't digest how God could allow this terrible disease to take part in your body. My thoughts were that you were a man of God, a faithful man, one who lived out what he preached and lived according to God's instruction and you had a disease that could possibly take your life. I was terrified, crushed, depressed and unsure of what to do with myself. All I knew was I had to take care of you. I had to be there for you every step of the way during that time because you were going to be okay. I immediately applied for FMLA at my job to ensure I was there to take you to your chemotherapy and radiation appointments. You were not going through this alone. I was going to be there for you, as you had always been there for me. I remember having to feed you through a PICC line because you weren't always able to eat. You couldn't tolerate solid foods. I was so proud to care for you. I cleaned the area and changed your dressings. I wanted to see you return to a healthy state. I watched you go through so much. I also watched you continue to encourage and be strong for many others. During your chemo sessions, you talked with the other patients and encouraged them, shared the word of God, laughed, talked and even prayed with and for them. You always kept your eyes on the promises of God. Although you were sick, and I could see what the cancer was doing to you, your faith never wavered, and you remained strong and firm in it. You trusted in God for the journey. I asked you why God would allow that to happen to you and your reply was, "Why not me?" You looked at it as another way to testify about God's grace and mercy.

During the months of July through November of 2009, we were out of church quite a bit. We returned to church on our Homecoming and you preached your heart out. You were cancer free and witnessed for The Lord, and you had a testimony. Life was back to normal for us and for you. We went to all your doctor's appointments to ensure you were feeling well and 2010 was great! I had my daddy back, and I bought a new house that year. I called an old friend and told him you weren't strong enough to get me moved into my new home alone and asked for his help. He showed up with a group of friends that moved the entire house, put up the beds and unloaded all the furniture, not to mention set it up, all for you, daddy. That year we began some traditions. On Wednesday's because I decided not to go to Bible studies, I cooked, and you came to my home afterward. And on Friday's we just hung out. Since I had my daddy back, I was going to cherish every moment and make some new memories.

The year 2011 came around quickly. I was laid off, but we had the best year. We shared the best times together, and I had a chance to hang near you the entire year. I took the kids to school every day, talked to you on the phone, went home and started my job search and to no avail, picked the kids up from school and came straight to your house. We'd hang out, cook, go out for meals and made great memories. We took the Disney World trip in July of that year. God put a ram in the bush and people blessed us with that trip. It was all God!

Later that year in 2011, as we prepared for a concert featuring you at TAB, we had so much fun at the rehearsals and fellowshipped with the other choir members. Our old choir director came back for the occasion because it featured you, this was something you wanted to do. I remember one rehearsal when you were not feeling well, and although you had a wedding dinner afterward, we left early. One thing you never did was complain, so if you said you were feeling bad, it had to be bad. That was in early October of 2011, so we made an appointment. You started feeling worse, and my biggest fear came true. The doctor told us that your cancer was back and more aggressive than before. My world crumbled before me at the very moment.

The concert on October 22, 2011, was AWESOME! Your vision and your songs all came to fruition. You did not feel well at all on that day, but you drank a 5-hour energy drink, and we went to the church. Everyone was so happy to see you and the choir was amazing! One song stood out, "I Won't Complain." And you sang it beautifully. I cried each time you sang that song. That night was so memorable, and I will never forget it. You, with the strength God gave you, preached your last sermon on October 23, 2011. Shortly after that, we were back at St. Thomas Hospital with you, because you began to decline.

I often think of the days momma and I would sit in the hospital room with you, and her song was "You Were Always On My Mind" and mine was "Cover Me." And you'd say, "Please turn that off. It's as if we had gone already and you were sick of the music. As the days passed and I watched you get weaker, my heart broke into little pieces, because I was losing you. On November 25, 2011, I witnessed a swift transition. I witnessed you wrestling with something. I saw you changing, and your last words were Grace and Mercy, and on November 26, 2011, God called you home.

My life hasn't been and never will be the same. You were the glue that held this family together. You were my best friend, my constant. Not a day went by without me seeing you or talking to you. I wanted to let you know that I have momma with me. I have taken care of her the best way that I know how because you were her world, but she now has me and the kids. Momma has been very strong, but without you, we can't do much with her daddy.

I have grieved every day. Some days are better than others. I have missed so many things about you. I don't have anyone to hold me and tell me everything is going to be alright anymore. I don't have a daddy anymore, no lap to sit on, no one to call me Bozo anymore and no one to love me unconditionally anymore. It's an open wound. Time heals all things, they say, but I don't know. What I do know for sure is I will keep leaning and depending on God's word. I want to see you again and cannot if I don't live for Christ, as you did. I strive to be all I can because I want you to be proud of me. I have made some mistakes, big ones, but I keep on pushing to be as great as you were daddy. I want to leave a legacy like the one you left, daddy. At your memorial service, one of the son's preached and said, "The best sermon that Pastor Hunt preached was the one that he lived."

Missing you Daddy, Chitquita

Dedication:

I would like to dedicate this chapter to the selfless, hardworking, strong, spiritual, phenomenal woman who is my mother, Nettye Hunt. Thank you for your love and support and for encouraging me to do anything that I put my mind to do. I would also like to dedicate this chapter to my friends who have lost their fathers, there is nothing like the love of a father.

Chitquita V Ward is a mother of two wonderful children and spends the majority of her time with her family. In her spare time, she likes to write novels, short stories, sing and travel with her family and friends. Chitquita holds a Bachelor's of Science Degree in Social Work with a minor in Psychology from Middle Tennessee State University. Currently, she is working diligently to have her first novel published.

A Simple Conversation

By Tonya Bays

Dear Dad,

A simple conversation is all I ever wanted ....

As a little girl, I often wondered why you were not there and what I did wrong. Oh yeah, I heard the stories of why, but I thought it would be befitting to hear it from you. Let's see-- I heard you were good and I heard you were handsome. I heard you were even a loving father to some. But the only regret is I didn't hear anything from you. The reason being because I have never had that conversation. As a little girl, I wondered if you knew anything about me. I wondered if you asked questions. I wondered if you even cared. I wished you would have wanted to get to know me. For years I dreamed of just one conversation that never happened. The conversation where you told me that you were sorry for not being there. You know the conversation where you called me your little girl.

Well, time has passed, and I'm all grown up now. Yes, I'm a parent with children of my own. You don't know much about me, but I have never been one to ask for much. If I could have just one wish concerning you, it wouldn't be that you raised me. It wouldn't be that we went to father-daughter dances. It wouldn't be that you held me in your arms and called me your precious baby. It wouldn't be that you taught me how to drive. It wouldn't be that you bought me flowers and told me how special I am. It wouldn't be that you complimented me on my beauty and admired me for my talents. If I had one wish concerning you, it would be simply for one conversation.

Some daughters want money. Some daughters want flowers. Some daughters want you to come into their life and prove your love to them. Some daughters want celebrations and laughs and walks in the park. All I wish for is one simple conversation.

In that conversation, I'd tell you how I had a pretty good life so far. I'd tell you how God sent a father into my life that I truly love. He raised me to be courageous. He raised me never to give up. He raised me to work hard. He taught me how to take care of the home. He taught me how to change a flat and check my engine oil because he wanted me to be safe. He bought me my first car and taught me how to keep it clean. Yes, he was strict, but he kept me in line. He disciplined me and taught me to be disciplined. He stood by me. There were times that I thought he didn't love me and that was when he proved it the most. He not only married my mom and got stuck with me but he adopted me both legally and emotionally. Many didn't understand because they thought why should you get that when others claim they were more deserving. I can only say what I'm sorry for; I understand the pain. I lived it in a different way. He taught me life lessons and passed on his wisdom. All I ever wanted from you was a simple conversation.

Maybe God gives us what we need regardless of what we want. Did you know that years later when there was no need to father me my dad still looks out for me? Yes! I can call on him anytime. He really cares for me and my children. Yes! I am a grandma now! And I am so blessed. I respect the role and importance of parenthood. I pride myself in loving my children. Yes. He was there to walk me down the aisle, and he kept me strong when I experienced my strongest battle. I remember his words. "Be strong" He stood with me at the grave site when I had losses. As an adult, he prays for me and talks with me and allows me to vent when I need to vent. The talk always ends with him reminding me that I am going to be alright and to just trust God. Can you believe he still sends me cards and gifts for birthdays and holidays? Yes, that conversation would be wonderful if we had it today. I could tell you that I wasn't a tem-porary situation for my father, but I am his daughter. He didn't just step into my life, but he stayed in my life. It would have been nice to tell you how blessed I am to have a father in my life. A father who now reminds me of what the Word of God says and encourages me through my tough times. So, all though you weren't there, and it seems like I may have missed out I can tell you, dad, thanks to my father I was never alone. I never went without and he has never left me. He is there when I call. He gives me a shoulder to cry on, and he loves me just as I am. I could tell you all of this if we just had one conversation.

If you were sorry that you were not there, I would be able to tell you that I was okay. I understand that people say blood is thicker than water. But my dad taught me that love is thicker than them all. I would let you know that my father raised me to forgive. He raised me to think positive. So, as I became an adult I never had any hard feelings toward you. I forgave you a long time ago. These are some of the things I would tell you during our conversation.

You know it wasn't always easy. As a kid there were times, I didn't always feel accepted. There would be seasons of instability. There would be seasons of silence and seasons of neglect. I know he didn't know it, but often people would tell me "you're not his, your skin is too dark, and your hair is too short." "You're not proper enough! "You don't belong. "And the one that hurt deeply "That's not your daddy" People only see what they want to see. During those times, though, I really wanted that conversation with you.

OH! I couldn't end the conversation without telling you how much I love my dad. Some people will never know how awesome he is to me. He is the father that I adopted long after he adopted me. I thank my dad for the memories he gave me. I remember playing basketball in the backyard. He was my coach. I remember where he would stand at every baseball and basketball game. He was a great supporter. I remember the long drives from state to state. We took family trips together. I remember when we would take dream drives where he would take us out and say "you can be anything you want to be. I remember homework nights and chores on Sat-urday. Every memory wasn't fun but necessary. I remember family games. Yes dad, in our conversation I'd tell you how even though you didn't raise me, I think you'd be proud of me.

My childhood was not perfect, but my dad was there. The funny thing is that I always knew he was the dad for me. See some people think that a "good" dad is one who does everything right. The one who looks the part; pun intended. I beg to differ a good dad is the one who is there who comes in your life and stays in your life. I can say through my child's eyes he didn't always seem like the perfect father growing up, but he is the perfect dad now. He is the one who came in my life and stayed in my life. These are the things I would tell you in my conversation.

Yes, that one conversation is all I ever wanted from you. Just a chance to sit and talk and tell you about my life. I know you wouldn't know everything by this simple conversation. But maybe enough to realize that if I wasn't enough for you to be there or enough for you to love, that I was at least enough for a simple conversation. Maybe we would have laughed or cracked a joke or two. Maybe you would have seen a glimpse of me in you. Yes, that is all I really wanted from you. It never seemed like too much to ask. At least--not until that sad day-- when I heard the news. The news that you had left this earth. I knew then I would never have that conversation, but I've always had a father.

Tonya Bays is a native of Alamo, TN. She presently lives in Milwaukee, Wisconsin. She has been married for 18 years and is a mother to four children. Tonya is an ordained minister, has a Master's Degree in Education and currently works as an 8th grade English teacher. She enjoys nature walks, teaching, and spending time with family.

Dear Daddy

By *Tammy Pullum*

Dear Daddy,

L et me start off by telling you that I miss you very much. I missed you while you were here, and I truly miss you more now than ever. I am writing you this letter more for me than for you. I hope it will be cathartic in helping me to forgive you and myself, and maybe bring some love and happiness back into my life. Daddy, I have some questions I need to ask you. Hopefully, you can help me find the answers. Even though you have been gone for a few years now, I'm hoping by composing this letter to you, I can gain some clarity about the relationship we had and the one we didn't have.

Daddy, If I can figure out why you weren't there for me, hopefully, I will be able to move through the hurt and pain, as well as forgive you and forgive others who have betrayed me. I can't continue to carry this burden because it is not mine to bear.

Dear Daddy, I am so lost today! Why did you divorce us, your five daughters, when you and mom divorced? We were innocent bystanders. We were casualties of the war between you and our mother. You were supposed to be a soft place to fall, a shoulder in which to cry. Why weren't you there for me? Why did you walk out to never look back? I was only ten years old at the time you left. Some days I still feel like that ten-year-old whose father walked out on her. I was your middle child, so very vulnerable and innocent, and needed you desperately.

Daddy, when you found out I was pregnant at fourteen, why didn't you come around to talk to me? Why didn't you at least call to check on the baby I was carrying and   the same town with me, and I didn't see, hide nor hear from you during that time. I needed you to reassure me that you had my back and that everything would be okay. I got nothing from you! Why Dad? Were you so disappointed in me that you deliberately stayed away? Did you forget that you got mom pregnant at fourteen? Your knowledge, wisdom, and guidance could have helped me understand what I was going through. But you never came by or called.

Daddy, where were you when I was forced to get married on my sixteenth birthday? Did you have any say in that arrangement? Did you stay out of it because my situation was a carbon copy of yours and mom's when you were both sixteen and eighteen? Did you feel in your heart that I was okay? I wish you would have felt every punch, kick, and lash with a belt that he gave me from age sixteen to seventeen. Well, maybe not every lash, because there were many, and I wouldn't wish that kind of pain on my worst enemy, nor my absentee father. Dad, I remember reaching out to you and telling you he was beating on me. Did you ever talk to him and tell him to stop hitting me? Apparently not because he didn't. I know you and I communicated somewhat during that time. Well, I guess it wasn't really communication. Every time you were the bouncer at the club when I came in you would give me a one-hundred-dollar bill and tell me to leave. I started going there when I was broke, just to see if you were there because I knew you'd give me the one-hundred dollars to get me out of there. By then I was seventeen and wasn't supposed to be in a nightclub by any means. However, I was alone and raising my two children, trying to keep food in their mouths and clothes on their little bodies. Those one hundred dollars came in handy and felt like a thousand dollars, back then, in the seventies. So, I want to thank you, Dad, for those times you were there. I guess I can say those were the most memorable times I ever shared with you. It's sad, don't you think, because we didn't have more of a father daughter relationship than that.

Speaking of relationships--Relationships!!! There have been many for you and myself. Most of mine were good. Mind you; I said most. Some were horrible, but I made it out alive. The good ones were good because I was the one calling the shots. I was the one in my own apartment and paying the bills before the relationship ever started, so I had total control. Things generally went my way, right? Why do I find myself at fifty-something in a relationship with no control? This is what I'm trying to figure out now. Why did I let myself go at this point in my life? Why do I feel so lost and alone now? I remember you always saying, "You can do bad by yourself." Most times throughout my life I was by myself. Just me and my four kids.

I left my home, my children, and grandchildren behind. I left all of my worldly belongings behind and just picked up and moved. I relocated from a big city to a two-block town in

Tennessee. What was I looking for? Was it love I never felt from you, Dad? Where is all that love, confidence, and wisdom you were supposed to give me? Did you take it with you? I could really use it now. I must have been looking for a replacement for you—maybe trying to fill the hole in my heart that you left. All I ended up with is a great big butcher knife stuck in my back-- a knife pushed so deep it is pierced down through both my lungs and my heart. But, I will not have it removed because I need it to serve as a reminder to me to never do this again, to never give up my freedom to a virtual stranger. Even though it's been eight years without a man in my life, was I so desperate for one? Was it those eight years without intimacy that made me think I could be safe and loved by a stranger, even though we have known each other since the early nineties?

Daddy, if you were still here would you have any answers for me? If you were still here would I be in this exact place in my life? I am trying to look deep into my soul to come up with reasonable answers for all of these questions. I am trying to convince myself that I'm not crazy or confused. It's hard, but I'm trying. Maybe I'm afraid of the answers, is why I haven't any. Maybe I know I couldn't control the promises he made to me to get me here and that I should have made him show me first. Hopefully, Dad, this will be one of the worst mistakes I ever make again, but probably not. I'm still human and imperfect no matter how hard I try to be a better person. One thing I know for sure today is, I made a life-altering decision and to change it I must put my big girl panties on and keep moving. No more crying over spilled milk. I was being told what I wanted to hear, and I took it and ran with it. I have to accept my responsibility in this situation and not blame him. He was just being himself. Talk about being funny. He can make me laugh so hard--when he wants too, till I almost pee my pants. That's one thing I remembered and loved about him from the past.

He could always make me laugh, and when we recently reconnected, he had me laughing from that very first text message to phone conversations. The sad thing I realize now is that laughter hides a lot of things. Laughter hides the things they don't want you to see. The darkness within that they try to camouflage. Even though a person is funny on the outside, you should always look deeper. Deeper on the inside is where the pain of the past lies. The only way to see it is with time. Time is what I thought I didn't have or need. Nevertheless, I was wrong. Now I see the real person whom I just don't see the laughter in anymore. The jokes have played out. It's like, "oops, my bad"!

Dad, if you were still here, what would you suggest I do? To give the relationship a fair chance to grow? Would you tell me when a man shows you who they are, you'd better be seeing him in that light? Would you tell me to take off the rose-tinted glasses I must have on and see with clear eyes? One of his favorite sayings is, "I can show you better than I can tell you." I believe now that this is my answer. He has shown me the man he is without the laughter to hide behind and that man I don't know. The very ugly attitude he is walking around with now, I have never seen before and cannot tolerate. That butcher knife that's sticking out of my back hurts but if I have it removed, I'm afraid I will repeat this behavior.

Will I ever be able to trust a man again? Will this wall of protection I have put up around me ever be penetrated? This wall I have built around me is so high, and so thick I don't think the next man will be able to get through it. Maybe that will be a blessing for me, or maybe my cross to bear and I will accept either.

I finally get it now, Dad! This letter to you was very cathartic for me. I believe I truly have my answers. I believe if you were here you would be very proud of me. If I hadn't addressed this letter to you, I don't believe I would understand what got me here. So, Dad, the last thing I want to say to you is, "Thank you". Thank you for not being there when I needed you to be. Thank you for not giving me that soft place to fall when I was fourteen and pregnant. I needed to go through all this pain and madness to come through the fire. Thank you for the scar tissue you have helped build around my heart as a reminder for me to keep moving forward. Thanks, Dad, for the courage and strength that is in my DNA from you that helps me keep pressing forward! I believe I have carried that around with me from the day you left me at ten years of age. You never looked back, and neither do I. I miss you Dad, with all my heart and please forgive me for not coming to see you when you were sick and for not coming to your funeral. I wasn't feeling anything for you back then, but this letter has helped me heal and forgive, and for this, I am truly grateful! I miss you Dad, and I believe one day, in the near future, we will see each other again. R.I.P!!!   Love always, Your, Tam Tam!!!

Tammy Pullum is the mother of 4 beautiful children, 8 beautiful grand-children, and an amazingly handsome great grandson. She is a graduate of Lincoln College with an Associate's Degree in Art History. Tammy has a love for art and is currently putting together a collection of paintings.

She has more than 25 years in the healthcare field as a Patient Care Technician, Medical Assistant, and most recently a Phlebotomist. Tammy currently resides in Friendship, TN after relocating from Tacoma, Washington. When she is not writing or painting, Tammy enjoys reading and has a guilty pleasure of reality television.

Questions and Time

By Cryss A. Jones

The following is a letter to my father, Christopher Columbus Jones, on the thirty-third year anniversary of his death.

Dear Daddy,

I never know where to begin. We've done this- well, I've done this every September 4th, since about 1985. Usually, I would tell you about the family, and give you world updates (trust me, you don't want to know); tell you how I continue to screw-up my life, etc., but not this time. I'm almost fifty (50) years old, and I have lived, learned, loved, and lost. I've had happy moments. I've had hellish times. I've laughed heartily, loved deeply, and managed to become a bit jaded, in the process. I have finally, FULLY surrendered my life to Christ, so my perspectives are ever changing. That said, I want to share a few things, muse a bit, and ask questions, say things I've not been able to admit, before now.

As I've grown older, it seems I have more questions than answers. I thought you were supposed to grow in wisdom, as you got older. I guess the nature of the questions prove that I have, in fact, become a little wiser. I supposed when you get near the fifty (50) year old mark, and you begin to ponder; seek deeper meaning. What have I done with my life? Have I made a positive difference in the world? Regrets? What's next? What is my relationship with God like? How long do I have left? Momma's gone now; two days before my birthday, nonetheless. Man, do I miss her. I'm widowed, with no children. The words family, legacy, and ancestry are now more than mere concepts.

Reminisce with me, Daddy. Lemon Street. 8-8:30 p.m. Momma would get me bathed, and in my pajamas, and I would anxiously await the sight of your big Lincoln Town Car coming down the street, to take me for my nightly ride around the block. I must have been about four years old when this blissful ritual began; at least that's my earliest memory. Your car seemed to take up the whole block; your presence, the entire neighborhood. People always stopped and stared, when you were around. You were, to me, larger than life. Always larger than life. I had no concept of the fact that you worked three jobs, seven (7) days a week, just to be certain that I had anything I wanted, and that you probably needed to be asleep at that time. You always made time for me. How? How did you do it?

Picnics at Robert E. Lee Park (Raa-baa-lee, as I called it), after you'd gone to Corned Beef Row, and got massive deli sandwiches, and everything to go with it. The movies, when you would put Planters peanuts in your Coke. Ice Cream floats; root beer for you, and grape for me, at Read's Drug Store, on a lazy Saturday afternoon. Taking me to work with you, to your day job, driving the Baltimore City Dental Bus to the elementary schools so that kids could have free dental care. First, we'd go to the small restaurant around the cornerfrom the bus garage on Elgin Avenue, or "go-rage," as you said in your southern accent. You'd have coffee, and, a chocolate cake donut, with milk. You always said that you liked "a little coffee in your cream and sugar." I drink it that way, too, on the rare occasions in which I indulge. It seemed every staff person recognized you, at your job, and always greeted you kindly, by name; Mr. Jones. They seemed to already know me, as well. You'd tell anyone who'd listen about me. Why? Afterward, we'd make our way to the garage, and greet your fellow drivers. They knew of me, as well. Ms. Marty, and Ms. Daisy, the Bus Aides, from when you used to drive a reg-ular school bus. "Are you paying attention in school, young lady?" "Make sure you're being a good girl. Your Daddy really loves his baby." I felt so special. But why so special to you? Why sacri-fice so much? You, and your best friend, Mr. Charlie Wilson, would go to your respective buses, after a bit of morning " jawing", and prepare for the day. I watched you intently. Your ritual the same. Every detailed etched in my memory. Open the bus doors, start theengine, turn on the lights. Starched navy blue uniform straight, one pant leg tucked into your work boot, and black leather work gloves; first left, then right. You would descend from the driver's seat, and begin taking the wooden blocks from each tire. You checked fluids, tire pressure, and gave the bus a thorough once over, before inviting me to my usual seat, where the kids would wait for their exams, and we were off.

"What school are we going to today, Daddy?" You'd answer, telling me which Dentist would be working that day, about how often you went to that particular school, and how great the hot lunch was, that was always waiting for you. No joke there. Those lunches were Amazing! The Bus Aides, female Teachers, and Cafeteria ladies LOVED my Daddy. I was too young to know how much, or why, though. Those "Jones Boys", they used to call you, and Uncle Shep. Every six months, I'd have my annual teeth cleaning. My eighth year stands out for me, as it was PURE HELL! During the visit, I screamed and cried out in pure agony, and you used to be so angry, and embarrassed by my behavior. The Dentist was Dr. Davis, a very mean caucasian man, who had a goatee, and looked as if he could be a villain on "Get Smart". He used to tell me to "stop all that shuckin' and jivin", or "shut up all that noise", but only when you were out of earshot. I thought he was your boss, and I didn't want you to argue with him, and maybe lose your job, because of me, so I began to tolerate pain, in silence. I remember him telling you that I had eight (8) cavities! I thought your head was going to pop off, and steam would come out. Too many cartoons, right? You even called me Crystal, that day. CRYSTAL. I didn't respond immediately, as it sounded so foreign coming from a man who'd only called me "Daddy's Baby". I knew two things in that moment: it was going to be a scarily quiet ride home, with no stop at the Sears and Roebuck on North Avenue for new doll clothes, and that you'd be gunning for my Momma.

I'd seen your temper (verbal) first hand, when it came to her. Whew! Your attack was fierce, frightening, all-consuming. When you told Momma, she was angry with me, too. An argument ensued; you blaming her for letting me eat so much candy, she blaming you for the same. I went to my hiding place under the table, until I thought it was safe to exist, again. It wasn't until I was 12 years old that a random conversation with Momma, led to the revelation that I had not been given a numbing agent, whilst the Dentist was drilling, and filling my teeth. I guess she told you, huh? The next time I saw Dr. Davis, he looked extremely nervous, and was very gentle. Go figure. You drove for the Baltimore City Schools, during the day, ran bus trips for Harford Motor Coach on weekends, and "hacked". I don't remember a time when you weren't there, and you lived clear on the other side of town. How, Daddy? How did you manage it all? Hugo Avenue. I recognized your signature "zing-zing" of our antique doorbell every single day. I waited all day for your visits. They were solace. They were safety. They were pure love for me -- for the weird kid no one liked. Most of the neighbors thought you lived with us, because you were there each day, after work. Houdini could have learned a few things from you.

I ALWAYS seemed to be asking for something. Late night trips to the house, because I had a nightmare; a trip across town, in a torrential downpour, because I'd heard a new song on the radio, and HAD to have the 45 r.p.m., THAT DAY ! "With A Little Luck- Paul McCartney, and Wings. Just for the record, Daddy, all of that had to hear the music, had to have it, turned out to be how I became a Songwriter, Singer and Composer, with perfect pitch. It wasn't wasted. I promise. It wasn't wasted, was it?

Expensive jewelry, dolls, souvenirs from your bus trips. All of this outside of the new wardrobe each season; Christmas, Easter, Birthdays, Halloween, Back-to-School-- Heck, you gave me my first diamond. A sterling silver necklace, with a cross, and a diamond chip in the middle. I fell in love with it, during one of our trips to the mall. You were looking at a necklace for yourself, because you always looked good, head-to-toe. Sharp as a tack, just to go around the corner. I begged and begged, with no idea that getting my necklace meant you didn't get yours. Why didn't you say "no", Daddy? Why was I always asking for something? I'd make up for it later in life, when I got a good job, though. We had time.

The ice rink. The 1980 Winter Olympics was the goal. Whether it was Northwest Ice Rink, Memorial Stadium, or Baltimore Gas, and Electric, we were there. Cold weather, low on money, exhausted, you got me there. It's one of the few things you and Momma tag-teamed on. I'd fly across the ice, with beautiful abandon, while you drank stale coffee, and watched. The expensive skates, lessons, ice time. I was gonna make you proud. I bet you knew all along, I was never going to make it to the Olympics, didn't you? I didn't have the feet, the flexibility, or the money. Why didn't you tell me?

I recall August of 1982, just before I began high school, you, Uncle Shep, and I went to visit your family in Virginia. I loved being with both of you, and the ride was scenic and the area unfamiliar, and exciting. We rode past vast fields of what you called "soldier beans". You would think an inquisitive kid like me. ALWAYS full of questions, would have been frantic to know every detail of your young life -- of both of your lives. Where did you play? Who were your friends? Where did you go for fun? When did your parents die? What were you afraid of, other than Squirrels (that still tickles me, tough guy)? Where were your parents buried? Did you cry? Who taught you the things that you know about cars? Who's your favorite Aunt, or Uncle? Did you get whippings, and for what? No. I asked NOTHING! Why? I was content just being with you. You were my deep breath. I didn't need to know a thing. After all, I could ask those questions when I grew up and had a family of my own. You weren't going anywhere.

Meeting your Cousin Easter was an absolute JOY. I was so shy, and so overwhelmed with the strangers about me, I was afraid to let you out of my sight. I slept on a fold-out bed, in a living room. The night seemed darker than black, and there was absolute silence. To this day, it's the best, and most peaceful night's sleep I've ever had. Remember breakfast, Daddy? I'd never had fried corn, and you had to coax me to eat. You cut my breakfast meat for me, as usual (yes, I was 14 yrs.

old), and I think you let me eat some pork, even though Momma never knew. I didn't care. As long as I had you in my line of sight, or could hear your voice, your booming laughter, my world was safe. You weren't gonna get too far. It was a wonderful trip. I still have the pictures, the memories--the, ahem, enough of that. was you. Here's what I've learned: 1- God actually loves me more than even you did. 2 -Take nothing, and NO ONE for granted. 3 - Want vs. Need. 4 - Love really IS the answer to all things, so don't sprinkle it, pour it. 5 - I will never believe that man, on that day, in that coffin You would NEVER abruptly leave me, at age 62. I wanted for your return from your trip to Boston. You were due back on Monday, Sept. 3, 1984. I spoke with you on Saturday, Sept. 2, 1984, for the last time. Did you know? You called me from your hotel room that night. In hindsight, you sounded woefully tired. I'd just come in from working an eleven(11) hour day at the shoe store, with Sharon. She would always let me work to earn cash for holidays, or back-to-school. I was absolutely exhausted. I rushed you off the phone. I needed rest. Besides, we had time to talk when you got back, right? Did you bring me a souvenir? I know you did you always did. When we were hanging up, you said, "Good-bye". How strange? You'd never said that before. I stared at the receiver, after you hung up. Huh? Well, I'll ask you in a couple of days, when I saw you. No, I wouldn't. I'd be too busy telling you about my first day of school, senior year, and whining because I didn't get to go to Boston with you. There would be time for questions about your trip, your experience, your life.

There was always going to be time for questions, for revelations, for shocking details, for laughter, for tears, for the day you saw me graduate - the day you walked me down the aisle - to tell my children about your life. There was going to be time. I'm sorry, we're out of time.

Cryss A. Jones has been writing since the age of eight. Beginning with poetry, and songs, Cryss found freedom and joy in music and written word, utilizing them as a means of communication, in a world which she felt invisible.

She later delved into Journalism in high school and college, and has hosted two popular internet radio shows, with another in the horizon. Cryss is the Owner of Collective Management Group (CMGMT), a company that provides Business Consultation for start-up non-and for-profit companies, a s well as Virtual Assistant services, and Social Media Marketing and Public Relations. Under the CMGMT umbrella are Collective Press, a self-publishing company, and "writer's hub" for information, and all things literature; The Collective Artist's Entity, a Music Publishing, Business and Talent Management Company for Artists across the spectrum; Collective Artistry Music, a burgeoning record label for her music, and the work of other Indie Artists; and LyfeSource, a Life Coaching and Strategy Company, that employs a Solution-focused paradigm, to assist people in need of direction and guidance.

Cryss' undergraduate, and graduate studies are in Psychology, and Human Service Administration.

Cryss is a Christian woman, who lives to utilize her God-given gifts to bless others, creating a ripple effect of positive change, love and peace.

A Testament of Love

By *Susanna Mason*

Opening Prayer:

Papa God,

As I tell my story, I ask for You to guide me with supernatural revelation, wisdom and understanding. I ask that every written word would bring honor to You first and also to my parents, despite any shortcomings or failures on their part or on my own. Teach us, Daddy, how to combat the lies of the enemy with the Truth of Your Word. Teach us how to love unconditionally as you first loved us. I give all glory and all honor for my life and testimony to You, Jesus now and forevermore.

"This also comes from the Lord of hosts; He is wonderful in counsel and excellent in wisdom."
~Isaiah 28:29 ESV~

"There is a generation rising that curses their fathers and speaks evil of their mothers. "
~Proverbs 30:11 TPT~

Susanna Mason

There are no perfect parents just as there are no perfect people because we have all, at some point, believed the enemy's lies, so all of our journeys should include forgiveness, healing and restoration in varying degrees. My personal story has less to do with the successes and failures of my mother and father as it does how I reacted to and internally processed all of the people, events and emotions in my life...the lies I chose to believe about myself, others and God.

"There is therefore now no condemnation for those who are in Christ Jesus."
~Romans 8:1 ESV~

The Lies
"But look, you are trusting in deceptive words that are worthless."
~Jeremiah 7:8 NIV~

The Rejection Lie
"But I am afraid that, as the serpent deceived Eve by his craft-iness, your minds will be led astray from the simplicity and purity of devotion to Christ."
~II Corinthians 11:3 ~

For her first 2 ½ years o f life, she was doted on and adored, but that all changed when baby brother was born. Upon arrival, it seemed that he had such a commanding personality and contagious charisma that he was able to capture the attention and affection of any audience with little effort. She had n ever b efore experienced such feelings of inadequacy and rejection and she had no idea how to cope with these new emotions. After all, it wasn't his fault that he was so stinking adorable, but she had to do something about it! She had in no way anticipated that her perfect family would be completely disrupted by such a cute little monster, not to mention that he had the curls atop his head that she so desperately longed for! What was it about this baby that inspired such adoration, and why did everyone act so differently around him? What was it that made everyone love him so much that they forgot she was even in the room? It was as if she had instantly and without warning been totally rejected and replaced! This pain was so intense at such a young age that she had no idea what to do with it, so she began to hide it down deep inside her heart and there began the construction of a great wall.

This is where all of our journeys begin, where we make a choice to either believe the lies that the enemy says about us or to believe what our heavenly Father says about us. As her parents were not believers at the time, she had no grid for understanding who God was or what He thought about her, so she did what she could to cope with uncharted emotional territory, she hid it far away from others, from herself and from God.

"My people are being destroyed because they don't know me..."
~Hosea 4:6a NLT~

This great wall that she was to build would be very tall, constructed of many different materials and would require a lifetime of maintenance in order to remain strong enough to protect her from the pain of further and continuous rejection. Now that she had embraced this lie of the enemy that told her that she would always be rejected, the other lies would come so much more easily and be even more believable than the first. It would become very easy for her to blame her parents for not choosing her or for picking a favorite child at all and she would soon begin to resent them as well as her baby brother. As this resentment was cultivated in her tiny heart, it turned into bitterness, anger and unforgiveness. It was at that point that she began to withdraw from her family. She became increasingly less affectionate and more guarded as the lie that she had embraced continued to be supported by her environment and experiences. She had, in fact, unintentionally opened a doorway into her heart to the enemy of her soul. By believing that lie, she had embraced rejection as her lot in life ignoring the fact that her loving heavenly Father was and will always be constantly in pursuit of her.

Many years later, she would be confronted by these same feelings when a picture was taken of her very own daughter at the birth of her son. That picture made her heart stop beating! The expression on her daughter's face brought all of those horrible feelings straight to the surface. Was her daughter having those same painful feelings of being replaced that she had so many years ago? The fear in her daughter's eyes told the story of her mother's life. What would this new addition mean to the family dynamic? Would he be the center of attention? Would he be cuter, funnier, more loveable? Worst of all, would her parents reject her to embrace him? She just couldn't bear the thought of her daughter having to go through any of those painful experiences in which she had become all too familiar.

"When the righteous cry for help, the Lord hears and delivers them out of all their troubles. The Lord is near to the broken-hearted and saves the crushed in spirit. Many are the afflictions of the righteous, but the Lord delivers him out of them all. He keeps all his bones; not one of them is broken."
~Psalm 34:17-20 ESV~

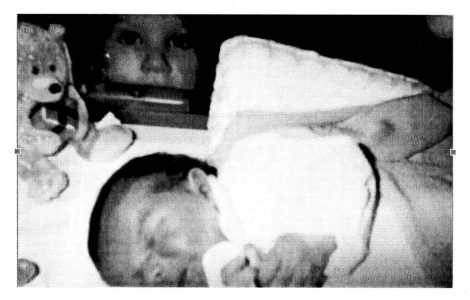

The Worthless Lie

"Therefore, if anyone is in Christ, he is a new creation. The old has passed away, behold, the new has come."
˜II Corinthians 5:17˜

"A lying tongue hates its victims, and a flattering mouth works ruin".
˜Proverbs 26:28 ESV˜

When she was usurped by this boy, the lie that she was not valued by others was reinforced in her mind and heart, and since she had already embraced rejection, the lie would slip in very subtly and almost without notice. Her worth and identity were now under siege by a ruthless enemy bent, ultimately, on murder.

Unfortunately, it is evidenced in the world we live in, that there is an inherent value difference between males and females. Gen-erally speaking, males have greater value in society than their female counterparts. These differences in value are just some of the many consequences of sin, specifically original sin. Even though God Created male and female to be equal partners in life, more lies of the enemy have distorted that reality and as a result, caused humanity to believe that women do not have the same value or worth as men. In the past, women have endured not having their voices heard or being able to vote. They have been paid less for doing the same jobs as men, as well as being passed over for jobs when equally qualified. This pattern of devaluing females has continued in families even as it is being addressed in society. There is nothing wrong with girls doing household chores, but when their brothers are not required to do those same tasks, it sends a message to the girls that boys are more valuable and should not be required to do medial household duties. It also sends an antithetical message to the boys that household chores are beneath them. This can cause much tension in a household stemming from a mother who may be overwhelmed with household chores, children and working a full-time job while her husband was raised to believe that doing "women's" jobs is beneath him and the precedent has now been set for their children, who are watching this dynamic play out daily in their own homes. As long as this behavior continues without interruption, the enemy will use it to reinforce the lies that he is perpetuating.

"For He Rescued us from the domain of darkness, and transferred us to the kingdom of His beloved Son."
~Colossians 1:13 NASB~

So, the lies that she has believed about herself are reinforced by what seems to her an unfair and biased favoritism towards her brother. He does not have to wash dishes or clean the house because these are female tasks and he is often allowed to watch television or play with his friends while she is required to do housework. She is blind to the fact that she is learning life skills by doing household chores, because she is consumed with the injustice of it all, continuously reinforcing her sense of worthlessness. Brother on the other hand is learning that he is very valuable to the family and to society and that his efforts would be better utilized elsewhere, but he is learning few life skills to assist him when he is grown and has a wife and a family of his own. So, the cycle continues with boys not being trained properly to become men, husbands and fathers as well as women lacking value and self-worth. Until exposed, these lies will continue to handicap individuals and families as they did her own.

The Unloved/Unlovable Lie
"We love because he first loved us."
~1 John 4:19 ESV~

"Anyone who does not love does not know God, because God is love."
1 John 4:8 ESV~

This lie is by far the most damaging an insidious of all of the lies that she believes because it will eventually rob her of her identity, sabotage her destiny and hijack her promises, at least for a time. The lies of the enemy, when believed, seem to build on one another and also to increase in power and negative consequences. The first lie of rejection leads her straight into the next lie of worthlessness which paves the road for her to believe that she is unloved and therefore unlovable.

Her father, although sweet and caring, is also very quiet and reserved. He is an amazing provider for his family, but he travels quite a bit in the military and then with his job, so he is not able to spend a great deal of time at home. She knows in her mind that he is supposed to love her, but she never feels his love in her heart or soul as she is unable to communicate with him effectively or really even get to know him. She is a verbal communicator, and he is definitively not. However, even though she longs for relationship with her Father and with others, she is somehow inept at conveying that need to any of them, so her desire for communication and relationship is repeatedly met with silence or disapproval both from within and outside of her family unit. Once again, these circumstances are feeding into the lies that she is rejected by others and worthless as well as introducing a new lie, that she may actually be unloved and therefore, unlovable.

Her father's father died when he was just 13 years old and she knows that it must have been terribly hard for him, but she does not understand why she has a living father who must not love her because he doesn't spend time with her or converse with her. She does not see the truth--that he struggles with relationships and communication with others due to events in his childhood. Instead, she believes that his lack of verbal communication and time spent together means that she was not worthy of his love.

Her mother, while the polar opposite of her father, still seems to have so many important things to do that she is too busy to spend time with her. After all, her mother has friends and housework and her baby brother to care for in addition to working. So, she ultimately spends a great deal of time playing alone or trying to find friends to play with or just watching a lot of television.

Her Mother also had traumatic events in her childhood, including an emotionally and often physically abusive father, which certainly affected her ability to relate to others. However, this was also misinterpreted as "My Mother must not love me because she does not spend time with me".

The enemy has set a trap for this child, beginning with rejection early in her life and moving to feelings of worthlessness and finally to believing that she is unloved because she is unlovable. She believes the lie that she is unlovable because if your parents can't love you, no one can, and she did not believe that they loved her. After all, they had rejected her and chosen her brother, they had enforced the standard of 'girl chores" making her feel devalued and now they did not spend time getting to know her, so they must not want a relationship with her. They must not love her--she must not be loveable. This was the only conclusion that was reasonable to her at the time--the only one that made sense given everything that had happened in her life.

There was also an incident of childhood fondling at age 8 by a boy that was a friend of the family that would serve to reinforce all of the lies floating around in her mind. If she was truly accepted, valued and loved, this would never have happened to her and she must never let anyone find out about it! However, this incident was very confusing to her because this boy couldn't possibly love her, or could he? After all, what was love? What did it look like? What did it feel like? Up to this point, she had never known love, so she had absolutely no grid for it. Maybe this was it maybe this boy WAS showing her acceptance, value and love. Or maybe it was another lie from an unknown, invisible enemy that was planning to take out his revenge on this unsuspecting child.

"Love is patient and kind; love does not envy or boast; it is not arrogant or rude. It does not insist on its own way; it is not irritable or resentful; it does not rejoice at wrongdoing, but rejoices with the truth. Love bears all things, believes all things, hopes all things, endures all things. Love never ends. As for prophecies, they will pass away; as for tongues, they will cease; as for knowledge, it will pass away."
~1 Corinthians 13:4-8 ESV~

The Plans of the Enemy

"The LORD told me about the evil plans of my enemies. That's how I knew about them. He showed me what they were doing. I had been like a gentle lamb that was led off to be killed. I

didn't realize they had made plans against me. They had said, "Let's destroy the tree and its fruit. Let's cut him off while he's still living. Then his name won't be remembered anymore." But Lord, you rule over all. You always judge fairly. You put people's hearts and minds to the test. So, pay them back for what they've done. I've committed my cause to you."
~Jeremiah 11:18-20 NIV~

Stolen Identity
"Before I formed you in the womb I knew you, before you were born I set you apart; I appointed you as a prophet to the nations."
~Jeremiah 1:5 NIV~

"Yet to all who did receive him, to those who believed in his name, he gave the right to become children of God."
~John 1:12 NIV~

The enemy now had her confused but still convinced that she was rejected by others and by God, that she was worthless to others and to God and that she was unloved by others and by God. He had laid a well thought out plan to destroy her life by stealing her identity, sabotaging her destiny and hijacking her promises and all before she even became a believer! After all, she would not believe in Jesus until age 12 so he would be ready to steal her identity before she even knew what it was!

One Wednesday night in January of 1983, she was in a class at church and had not been paying attention to the teacher, so when her friend next to her raised her hand, she did too. She did not want anyone to know that she was not really interested in anything except the fun games they played before class. After class was over, the teacher sat down with both of them and thanked them for rais-ing their hands and for wanting to accept Jesus as their Lord and Savior. She did not understand what that meant and was still convinced that God didn't love or accept her, but who was this Jesus guy, anyway?

She prayed with the teacher although she wasn't really sure what was happening or if Jesus could love her, when no one else did, or if she even believed in Him. She wasn't positive that this salvation thing actually took because she had not raised her hand in belief of Jesus, but only because her friend did...so had she really believed? The enemy would continue to implant those kinds of questions in her head causing her to doubt her salvation for many years to come.

However, the hand of God was on her life even then because she could not contain her excitement at her new-found salvation and was soon baptized with water to seal that decision. She also told her family about this Jesus she had met and in time, they all believed as well. However, this initial excitement soon wore off and because she had no idea how to connect with God on an intimate and personal level, she was unable to find acceptance, value and love, despite her continued searching.

As is so common in churches today, she was evangelized to the point of salvation, but never further taught, discipled or mentored into relationship with God Himself. She had once heard it said that Christianity was not about religion, but about relationship. She wanted desperately to understand what that meant? There just had to be something more to this relationship with God idea, but it continued to elude her. How can you have a relationship with a God that you cannot see or touch, when you don't even know how to have one with the people around you that you can see and touch and even converse with?

Now saved but still doubting her salvation and still damaged and confused by the lies of the enemy, she went through Middle and High School always searching for acceptance, worth and love wherever she could think to look, never wanting to admit that she couldn't find them on her own and never looking to God to meet all of her deepest needs. This probably looked like attention seeking to others, but she did not understand why no one seemed to love her.

"God said to me once and for all, 'all the strength and power you need flows from me', and again I heard it clearly said, 'all the love you need is found in me', and the Almighty said, 'the greater your passion for more, the greater reward I will give you."

~Psalm 62:12 TPT~

Sabotaged Destiny

"For still the vision awaits its appointed time; it hastens to the end—it will not lie. If it seems slow, wait for it; it will surely come; it will not delay."

~Habakkuk 2:3 ESV ~

"For those whom He foreknew, He also predestined to become conformed to the image of His Son, so that He would be the firstborn among many brethren;"

~Romans 8:29 NASB~

Her entire identity and destiny as well as the promises that God had spoken over her life were now in jeopardy as she was being pursued by a vengeful enemy and he was not trying to simply make her life tough, he wanted her dead. He had completely planned out her emotional, spiritual and physical destruction. His plan began to unfold with the lies that he told her. Once she had believed those lies, he would steal her identity in Christ before she ever figured out who she was or to whom she belonged. He would do this by planting doubts in her mind of her own Salvation and by never allowing her need for love, acceptance and worth to be fulfilled. His plan would then focus on the destiny that she carried as well as on the promises that were her birthright in Christ.

Because her behavior was flirtatious and overtly sexual due to not having a relationship with her parents, she was frequently rejected and judged by the religious community as well as the non-re-ligious community.

Much like the Samaritan woman at the well in John chapter 4, she was despised because of her position in society and because of her sinful ways. Absolutely no one, including herself, saw her potential or believed that she could be redeemed. In fact, no one ever reached out to show her the love of God. She would have to search it out on her own until she found it and it would require an actual encounter with Love Himself for her to be rescued from the snares of the enemy of her soul.

This behavior and the corresponding judgment and rejection by others continued and seemed to her to be further evidence of the lies of rejection, unworthiness and being unloved-unlovable. After all, there was no evidence to the contrary that she could discern. These lies essentially became the entire belief system that she used to get through life and to make all of her decisions, which led to some crucial mistakes, including unintentional pregnancies and emotionally and/or physically abusive relationships and marriages. However, her destructive lifestyle would prove to be the catalyst that would someday launch her out of the grips of the father of lies and into the loving arms of her heavenly Father.

"For we are God's masterpiece, created in the Messiah Jesus to per-form good actions that God prepared long ago to be our way of life."
~Ephesians 2:10 ISV~

Hijacked Promises
"And we know that for those who love God all things work to-gether for good, for those who are called according to his purpose."
~Romans 8:28 ESV~

At the age of 17, she was involved in a horrific car accident that should have killed her. She was an inexperienced driver traveling at a high rate of speed when she rolled a car 1 ½ times over a barbed wire fence, landing on the roof of the car in a ditch. Earlier that day, she had experienced a foreboding feeling which indicated that something terrible would happen, but with no other information than this strange sensation, she went about her day as normal. The accident occurred later that evening and when she walked away unharmed from a car that was totaled, she knew that God had been trying to prepare her for this event and protect her in it. Now, the enemy had attempted to take not only her emotional and spiritual capacities but her physical life as well. God intervened, and she walked away with a scratch on her hand, to remind her that He was not finished with her and that the enemy could not destroy His plans for her life.

"For I know the plans I have for you,' declares the Lord, 'plans to prosper you and not to harm you, plans to give you hope and a future."
~*Jeremiah 29:11 NIV*~

Despite her flirtatious behavior, she had one boyfriend all through high school that she was sure didn't really love her, despite his continued efforts to show her that he did. She believed that eventually, he would see that she was worthless and unlovable, and would reject her like everyone else had, so she broke up with him regularly before he had a chance to hurt her.

After their final break up and on her graduation night, at 18 years old, her virginity was stolen from her simply because she was so hungry for love and acceptance and so afraid of rejection that she simply could not refuse the dare of a drunk boy at a party. Soon after this event, her belief in the lies and the corresponding confusion that ensued would put her in a downward spiral of promiscuity, drugs and alcohol. These were just a few of the means that she used in her attempts to satisfy this ever-elusive need for love, acceptance and worth. These avenues, of course, proved unfruitful and would soon lead her into other things such as poor relationship choices, overspending and addiction to food in order to somehow gain comfort and relief from the ongoing emotional pain that was her life. Despite knowing that none of these things would provide her with any lasting joy or happiness, she continued some of her destructive behaviors well into adulthood, with brief respites where she truly sought a relationship with God. It was in these short periods of seeking a relationship with Him, that she would experience the most growth of character and personal breakthrough, but she was never able to remain intimate with God or focused on that relationship for any length of time, and she never experienced any true freedom from bondage.

"Above all, keep loving one another earnestly,
since love covers a multitude of sins."
~1 Peter 4:8 ESV~

The Plans of God

"The Spirit of the One who raised Jesus from the dead is living
in you. So the God who raised Christ from the dead will also
give life to your bodies, which are going to die. He will do this by
the power of his Spirit, who lives in you."
Romans 8:11

Heart of Stone

Believing the lies about herself, others and God, made her constantly feel rejected, worthless and unloved. These lies became the foundation for the wall that she would construct around her heart that was so thick and so tall that no human would ever get in. Somehow, she managed to keep everyone that should have cared about her at bay, destined to live on the outside of the wall and never truly knowing who she was. After all, she didn't know who she was, so how could anyone else?

Through unplanned pregnancies and failed marriages, she continued to maintain superficial relationships with others. But tired of never knowing or being known, and realizing that being alone would be better than the torture of a loveless marriage, she would leave her second husband in 2010.

Her heart wall had thickened, and her heart had grown cold inside of marriages where she felt completely alone, abused, rejected and unloved. She often wondered to herself, 'will I ever laugh or cry again? Will I ever feel anything again? Will I ever love or be loved?'

"I will give you a new heart and put a new spirit in you; I will
remove from you your heart of stone and give you a heart of flesh."
~Ezekiel 36:26 NIV~

Baptism in the Holy Ghost

"Likewise the Spirit helps us in our weakness. For we do not
know what to pray for as we ought, but the Spirit himself inter-
cedes for us with groanings too deep for words."
~Romans 8:26 ESV~

In 2001, upon the advice of a friend, she had begun to pray for the gift of tongues, just out of curiosity and not understanding that she would first need to be Baptized in the Holy Ghost. After praying for that gift for ten years, she finally decided that she must not be worthy of it and gave up praying. At some point, she began to understand that she needed to be baptized in the Holy Spirit in order to receive the gift of tongues. She was so relieved to know that she had not been deemed unworthy by God but that He had, in fact, heard her prayers and answered them.

In 2011, during her 5-year separation and bitter divorce process, she would in desperation, open her heart enough to finally understand that there was more to Christianity than sitting in a pew on Sundays and trying to no avail to be a good person. It was during that time, that she was finally Baptized into the Holy Spirit. This indwelling of the Spirit of God would soon begin the process of softening her heart and drawing her into a relationship with the lover of her soul.

Unfortunately, many churches in American culture do not teach new believers about the Baptism in the Holy Spirit, thereby denying them access to the power that comes when God lives inside of His children. We must, therefore be diligent to read and study God's Word for ourselves so that we are not deceived by the enemy or denied access to the promises and power that is found in God's Word.

It would take several more years after her Baptism in the Holy Spirit for the gift of tongues to fully manifest, but she then understood that prayer, studying God's Word for herself and faith in His plan and His timing was tantamount to coming into a relationship with Him. She was just beginning to believe that God may actually accept her just the way that she was and also that He loved her so much that He did not want to leave her in that painful place. She also began to believe that He would help her make the necessary changes in her life. For the first time, she was not alone, and her hope was being restored.

"But you will receive power when the Holy Spirit has come upon you, and you will be my witnesses in Jerusalem and in all Judea and Samaria, and to the end of the earth."
~Acts 1:8 ESV

Combating Lies with Truth
"For we do not wrestle against flesh and blood, but against the rulers, against the authorities, against the cosmic powers over this present darkness, against the spiritual forces of evil in the heavenly places."
~Ephesians 6:12 ESV~

The Truth
"Jesus answered, 'I am the way and the truth and the life. No one comes to the Father except through me."
~John 14:6 NIV~

Once she was introduced to the Indwelling Holy Spirit, she began to desire a relationship with Him, which included all members of the Trinity, Father, Son and Holy Spirit. She also began to sense His presence inside of her and while she was more aware of her own sin, she was not condemned by it, but instead was remorseful yet much more able to receive forgiveness. She began to fall in love with the Word of God and the Truth that it contained. Prior to receiving the baptism in the Holy Spirit, she would read the Bible and it would seem like just words on a page. Every now and then, the Lord would make those words come alive for her, but usually, it was as if she was just reading a history book. Now she reads the Bible and it touches her so deeply that she cannot hold back tears and she is literally being transformed by the power of the living Word. Her mind is continuously being renewed by the power of the truth of the Word of God, as she comes deeper into relationship with Jesus Himself.

In 2013, she began to get a sense of discontentment with her current situation and location. She had been asking the Lord to allow her to attend a School of Supernatural Ministry so that she could learn how to move in the different gifts. She was still in the middle of a divorce and was hearing that she needed to focus on moving forward with the Lord's plans for her life, as she had felt weighed down by the marriage and stressed by the difficult divorce. She was now committed not only to relationship with God but to learn-ing to hear His voice better and, so she entered into a Spirit led, 60 day directional fast. Despite everyone's warnings about entering into a fast consisting of only water and a variety of fruit and vegetable juices, she knew that she had received confirmations of the fast from the Lord and that if He was in it, He would give her the grace to do it. Her fasting prayers included requests for a job in the city where He wanted her to move and she really wanted to live on the beach, so she applied for jobs mostly in those locations. She had a pretty good job and a decent paycheck at Vanderbilt Hospital at the time and was just really feeling the prompting of the Lord to move. She had no idea for 59 of those days where she would end up going but she consistently held to the fast and on day 59, she got a job in Florence, Alabama. She had been to a couple of powerful conferences there and had felt very loved and accepted at the church where the conferences were held, so she was excited about starting over in a new town with a church family that had no preconceived ideas or judgments about her or her past. She also found out that the new church had a 3-year School of Supernatural Ministry that was much more affordable than the one available at her current church. She had no idea at that time, the journey of healing that was ahead of her, nor how the Lord would lead her and provide for her with every step she took. She was just so excited to venture out with the Lord and to step out in faith knowing for the first time, that He was leading her into her destiny--the same destiny that the enemy had tried so desperately to sabotage! She was beginning to understand that applying the truths of God's Word to her life with noticeably sanctifying results, was attainable only inside of a relationship with Jesus, The Way, The Truth and The Life. She was completely unable to live the Christian life apart from walking with and abiding in Him and she was no longer interested in any futile attempts at faking it.

"Sanctify them by the truth; your word is truth."
˜John 17:17 NIV˜

God Accepts Her
"For he chose us in him before the creation of the world to be holy and blameless in his sight."
~Ephesians 1:4 NIV~

The job, the move, the new schools for her and her two young children--everything happened so quickly that she barely had time to adjust to all of the changes. The children had an even harder time adjusting because they were still reeling from the separation and pending divorce, and now a completely new environment where they knew very few people and no one outside of our small church. They had moved just in time for the children to start a school year and she had to drop her son off every morning crying because he didn't want her to leave him.

Her daughter put on a much tougher façade but admitted later that she was dealing with some pretty hateful bullying and name calling that year. However, they soon began to settle into their new life and they were all learn-ing and growing so much at their new church that the attempts of the enemy to discourage them were futile. They all felt loved and accepted and each of them began to develop a personal and inti-mate relationship with the Lord. Both children were soon baptized in the Holy Spirit and the healing hand of the Lord became evident in each of their lives. This new church had immediately embraced her and her children without any knowledge of them or any expectations from them. She had finally found a group of people who really believed the Word of God and treated others accordingly. For the first time in her life, she truly felt accepted by other believers and by God. However, she still had a massive wall around her heart and continued to struggle with being vulnerable with God and with others and was highly susceptible to symptoms of loneliness and depression as a result. It is one thing to know in your head that God and others love and accept you, but never to know it in your heart because of the fear of further pain and rejection. She couldn't believe it, because she would not allow that wall of fear to be torn down so that God could come in and heal and restore her heart. But her heavenly Father is very patient and always pursuing relationship with her. She was learning that He would never leave her or forsake her and that He would heal the wounds of her childhood that continued to plague her well into adulthood. After all, He accepted her just as she was, and loved her too much to leave her that way. For her, it was always a matter of believing His Word so that her mind could be further renewed and transformed into the mind of Christ. Even while writing her story, her heavenly Father was healing places in her heart that had been locked away--dark places that were desperately crying out for the Light of God to shine on them, exposing them to the elements in order to break and remake them into something beautiful.

"The Spirit of the Lord God is upon me, because the Lord has anointed me to bring good news to the poor; he has sent me to bind up the brokenhearted, to proclaim liberty to the captives, and the opening of the prison to those who are bound; to proclaim the year of the Lord's favor, and the day of vengeance
of our God; to comfort all who mourn; to grant to those who mourn in Zion– to give them a beautiful headdress instead of ashes, the oil of gladness instead of mourning, the garment of praise instead of a faint spirit; that they may be called oaks of righteousness, the planting of the Lord, that he may be glorified."
~Isaiah 61:1-3 ESV~

God Sees Her Worth
"For you formed my inward parts; you knitted me together in my mother's womb. I praise you, for I am fearfully and wonderfully made. Wonderful are your works; my soul knows it very well. My frame was not hidden from you, when I was being made in secret, intricately woven in the depths of the earth. Your eyes saw my unformed substance; in your book were written, every one of them, the days that were formed for me, when as yet there was none of them."
~Psalm 139:13-16 ESV ~

"I give them eternal life, and they shall never perish; no one will snatch them out of my hand."
~John 10:28 NIV~

The School of Supernatural Ministry was an integral part of her personal healing journey. This was where she began to learn about her own identity in Christ. She read books and received teaching that she never before had access to. She was encouraged to explore her own creative outlets with speaking, writing, poetry and painting as well as music and worship. She was taught about the different gifts and was able to practice moving in Words of knowledge, Wisdom and Prophecy in an environment where she was never condemned for failure, but was encouraged to keep trying. It was during that time that she also received the gift of tongues and began to practice it daily for her own personal edification and encouragement. She had never known the kind of freedom that these believers enjoyed on a daily basis and she was soaking it all in. She began to realize some of her own talents and gifts and the creativity that she did not think she possessed emerged in new and different ways. Her fellow students and teachers also declared each other's worth as they were learning the creative importance of the spoken word. She learned to decree and declare the truths of God's Word over her life and the lives of her children. She was learning so much and was beginning to understand that the Lord created her in His image and therefore, she has worth. He saw her as worthy of His death on the cross. He wouldn't have died for someone that had no worth. He also had a plan and a destiny for her life that included spreading the Gospel of Truth to all the earth, as well as unity in the body of Christ and unity in relationship with God, just as the Trinity is unified, we also will be unified by God, for the purpose of bring-ing the kingdom of heaven to earth. We are the army of the living God and He is raising us up to fight on our knees for the benefit of the entire world.

Jesus Prays for All Believers

*My prayer is not for them alone. I pray also for those who will
believe in me through their message, that all of them may be one,
Father, just as you are in me and I am in you. May they also be in us
so that the world may believe that you have sent me. I have given
them the glory that you gave me, that they may be one as we are one
—I in them and you in me—so that they may be brought to complete
unity. Then the world will know that you sent me and have loved
them even as you have loved me."*
~John 17:20-23 NIV~

God Loves Her

*"Who shall separate us from the love of Christ? Shall trouble
or hardship or persecution or famine or nakedness or danger or
sword? As it is written:
"For your sake we face death all day long;
we are considered as sheep to be slaughtered."
No, in all these things we are more than conquerors through him
who loved us. For I am convinced that neither death nor life, neither
angels nor demons, neither the present nor the future, nor
any powers, neither height nor depth, nor anything else in all creation, will
be able to separate us from the love of God that is in Christ Jesus our
Lord."*
˜Romans 8:35-39 NIV˜

*"Therefore, as God's chosen people, holy and dearly loved, clothe
yourselves with compassion, kindness, humility, gentleness and
patience."*
˜Colossians 3:12 NIV˜

She has finally begun to experience life in the Spirit, life apart from rules, rejection and religion. Her journey of discovery has now led her back to the beginning--to the everlasting, eternal, I AM. Although she spent her life searching for love, acceptance and worth in all the wrong places, she would in fact, stumble upon the relationship that she so longed for in the One that she held at bay for so long. When she stops believing the lies and allows herself to be encountered and transformed by the Way, the Truth and the Life, she begins to see herself as loved by God, her heart opens up to Him and spiritual, emotional and physical healing become available and accessible to her! She also is given a strong desire for deep and intimate relationship with her creator and an understanding that she would literally not make it without Him. Her priorities would have to change because this transformation would require commitment and focus, however, once she desired Him above all else, He would do all the hard work necessary in her mind, heart and body.

During her time in the Supernatural School of Ministry, she attended a Sean Bolz conference where she had an encounter with Love Himself. She was in worship and while her eyes were closed, and she was fully immersed in praising God, a man with a beard came up and kissed her on her cheek. She never opened her eyes and had no idea who the man was, but what she did know was that the Lord Himself had somehow supernaturally poured His love out on her that night and as He did, she could feel herself being changed. She immediately felt covered and protected in Love and she knew that nothing would ever be the same for her. Prior to this experience, her independence had always kept her believing that there were some things that she could and should do without God, which is partly why she struggled so much at having a consistent ongoing relationship with Him. She also never believed that God loved her before now. However, she now knows without a shadow of a doubt that God loves her and that He stepped down from heaven to place a supernatural kiss on her face. She finally understands that He loves her and that she can do NOTHING apart from Him, but ALL THINGS with Him. She is unable to survive any longer outside of relationship with God. In fact, it is His power dwelling in her that enables her to breathe. There is no turning back now that she has discovered that playing games with God only delays her blessings and her breakthrough. She is finally fully committed to abiding in Him and dwelling in His presence because she at last knows in her heart the depths of His love for her. She has experienced the everlasting love of God and she is immediately and forever changed by this encounter.

"I am the vine; you are the branches. Whoever abides in me and I in him, he it is that bears much fruit, for apart from me you can do nothing."

~John 15:5 ESV~

"We demolish arguments and every pretension that sets itself up against the knowledge of God, and we take captive every thought to make it obedient to Christ."

~2 Corinthians 10:5 NIV~

"See to it that no one takes you captive through hollow and deceptive philosophy, which depends on human tradition and the elemental spiritual forces of this world rather than on Christ."
~Colossians 2:8 NIV~

She had believed the lies that said she was unloved, unworthy and unaccepted for so long that the Truth would come by process and over time. However, it would be a process that she didn't even realize was happening until she was able to look back and see the changes that had taken place within her. As she tells her life story, she is transparently aware that her journey is far from over, and that she will always need the indwelling power of the Holy Spirit in order to continuously combat the lies of the enemy. However, she is also aware that she is completely accepted, full of purpose and deeply loved by God. She must continuously learn and embrace the Word of God in order to come against the lies that the enemy regularly attempts to speak over her. But as she embraces God and believes in His Word and trusts in His love for her, the enemy becomes powerless and she is transformed into the image and likeness of Jesus, just as He intended and purposed at creation. This transformation will always require the power of the Holy Spirit in you teaching you how to embrace the truth in order to be changed by it. God desires relationships with His children, so He will pursue relationships with us, but He will never overtake our will or try to control us in any way. He will gently lead and guide us into the understanding that He loves us and wants to be involved in our lives through a relationship. As she looks back on her life, she finally understands that each event that occurred was not to hurt, reject or torment her, but was simply to show her how much she needed God and how completely He would provide for her, within an intimate relationship.

"The coming of the lawless one will be in accordance with how Satan works. He will use all sorts of displays of power through signs and wonders that serve the lie, and all the ways that wickedness deceives those who are perishing. They perish because they refused to love the truth and so be saved. For this reason God sends them a powerful delusion so that they will believe the lie and so that all will be condemned who have not believed the truth but have delighted in wickedness."
~2 Thessalonians 2:9-13 NIV~

"Beloved, do not believe every spirit, but test the spirits to see whether they are from God, for many false prophets have gone out into the world. By this you know the Spirit of God: every spirit that confesses that Jesus Christ has come in the flesh is from God, and every spirit that does not confess Jesus is not from God. This is the spirit of the anti-christ, which you heard was coming and now is in the world already. Little children, you are from God and have overcome them, for he who is in you is greater than he who is in the world. They are from the world; therefore they speak from the world, and the world listens to them."
~1 John 4:1-6 ESV~

"For we know, brothers and sisters loved by God, that He has chosen you."
~I Thessalonians 1:4 NIV~

Dedication:

To my Father:

You were a great role model and a quiet, caring and consistent presence in our lives. Much appreciation for your bravery and hero-ism during your many years of service to our country in addition to your family. Most importantly, I thank you for seeking God in everything--we were watching and listening, even when you didn't think we were paying attention! I am so thankful for and blessed to have you in my life, because even though this life brings with it much sorrow, you always cling to Hope Himself! May you always know how much you are loved and appreciated each and every day!

I love you, Papa

"Honor your father and your mother, so that you may live long in the land the Lord your God is giving you,"
~Exodus 20:12 NIV~

Susanna Mason

To my Mother:

I have so much admiration for your many varying talents and abilities--your creativity and sense of style make me want to create and accessorize, your humor inspires me to laugh more and your love for family and friends makes me want to treasure and protect those relationships in my own life. I want you to know that although we do not always see things through the same lenses, I truly appreciate your unique perspective. I am so thankful for your influence in my life because it is those joyful, carefree footprints that you were making in the lives of those around you that enabled you to create a lifetime of memories for us all.

I love you, Mama

"Her children arise and call her blessed;
her husband also, and he praises her."
~Proverbs 31:28 NIV~

Susanna Mason was born to an American military family stationed in West Germany. She grew up in both South Carolina and Tennessee. She now resides in Alabama and is a single Mother of three and aspiring writer. After years of feeling rejected, unloved and unworthy, and further crippled by the judgment of others, shame and addiction, she was taken on a healing journey for the truth which included amazing encounters with the Lover of her soul. Her heart is currently under radical construction with the goal of total transformation. (Isaiah 61:3 TPT)

Letters to My Father is her first collaborative endeavor but future projects are beginning to materialize.

Loved & Chosen

1 Thes. 1:4

Lucanna Mason

While You Still Have Time

By *Love Brown*

L ouis Brown Jr or Buddy Brown to the locals was born March 13, 1937, to the late Ionia and Pittman Brown in Lauderdale County, Tennessee--poor country folks during the Great Depression. They were a family with ten children, which made the struggle even worse. So as many people then in those days, they got by as sharecroppers, hunting for food and gar-dening. Being that my father was born in that era, his way of life never faded. He didn't have much, so the desire was never there to obtain much as an adult. He fathered 13 children, and I also had two older siblings.

After he united with my mother, the struggle continued a fam-ily of 6 by that time. My mother had little education as well, so she never obtained a steady job and my dad relied on social security due to arthritis. Most summers our meals consisted of fish that we caught and chopping cotton and winters we ate mostly rabbits and my dad would haul wood for people for money.

One thing my father taught us was how to survive off the land, but he would also show us what a mean person he could be. He was very controlling and set in his ways. We all obeyed him including my mother because we knew we would suffer the consequences if not. He was an alcoholic and would come home many nights in a fit of rage. He would physically abuse our mother for no reason at all. And we would get our fair share of whippings too. Sometimes he would kick us out the house, but we would always go back. Many nights we would lie in our beds listening to the hurtful sounds of the lashes he would give to mom and her cries. We lay there helpless, too frightened to say anything out of fear of what he'd do to us. And this went on for as long as I could remember, throughout my entire childhood.

My oldest brother Frankie escaped to the Marines right after high school. When my sister Jennifer graduated, she left to live with our grandmother, and my brother Tony also joined the military. This left me home with my mother where I continued to witness the abuse until I graduated.

A few years later, I married and moved away, but eventually went back after becoming pregnant with my first child. My mom wanted me close to her, and in November 1999, my child was born and brought so much joy into the home. She was my parents first and only grandchild they shared together so they both adored her. My dad even came to the hospital with us when I had her. And things were good, or so I thought.

Time went on, and things turned for the worse once more and the final time. It was a cold December night close to Christmas. My dad arrived home very late and intoxicated. He started a fight with my mother which woke me out of my sleep. I could hear her crying and him yelling at her. He was telling her to get up, which I learned later that she was on her knees praying for God to put an end to this. And that enraged my father even more to the point that he got his shotgun and was threatening to kill her. I just couldn't take it anymore. I had enough of the torment and tried to go into the room to get my mom out of danger, but the door was locked. I knocked and called out to her, "Momma, are you okay! She kept telling me yes, and for me to go back to sleep. I kept knocking and twisting the knob until I heard my dad cock the shotgun and say "GET away from the door or I'll blow your damn brains out!". And even though I was afraid, I didn't move. I couldn't leave her in there. When the gun cocked, I knew he'd kill me, my mom, or possibly both. My mom kept praying to God; she said she looked up at my dad and couldn't recognize him as if the devil had completely taken over him. Then "SUDDENLY," a silence filled the house, and he allowed my mother to leave unharmed. Nothing but God!!

It had begun to snow, and in the middle of the night, me, my one year old child, my husband and my mother fled with nowhere to go. Soon we found a small home to live in, and we had to regain everything and start over. We were content nevertheless because we were out of harm's way. But after a while, my dad started to come by to visit my mom. I was so full of anger towards him that when he would come to the house, I would go into my room and shut the door. For over a year, I refused to speak to him or have a relationship with him at all. My mom saw the pain that I was causing him, and sat me down and explained to me that I needed to fix it. He was still my father and despite the awful things he had done in the past he was sorry for it and I needed to find it in my heart to forgive him.

Well in my own time, because I could be just as stubborn as my dad. I began to talk to him again. And after a while, we became closer than we ever had been before. He was then the father I always needed. He became this caring person. I saw a side of him that I never had before. He spent time with his then two granddaughters. He took them on fishing trips and loved to watch them actually catch one. He'd smile and laugh, and they made him so proud. He would get them Christmas presents, went to school programs, especially grandparent's day. He even went to a couple of basketball games. All the things he didn't do with us, he made up for it through them.

Then in 2014, tragedy fell upon us as my father was diagnosed with Stage IV brain cancer that had already spread throughout his body. His health condition declined so rapidly, and as I watched him get weaker by the day. I soon realized that my time with him was limited. I prayed for him but not for God to prolong his life. I knew he was suffering and that was no way to live in misery or pain. He had been such a strong-willed man his entire life and able to do anything and now he could barely walk. He had no appetite and towards the end, lost sight in one eye. His body was becoming frail and he spent most days lying on the couch sleeping.

His last day of treatment we noticed that he was becoming more short of breath. He was hospitalized with a diagnosis of radiation pneumonia, and his heart was failing. As I sat there by his side, my heart ached. I wasn't prepared for this and certainly not ready to let him go. He had taught me so many things, but he hadn't taught me how to live without him. He would occasionally wake up and look over at me, and I'd hold his hand to let him know I'd never leave his side. I was there for him as he had been for me. While at the hospital, an altercation occurred between my mother and his mistress which lead to mother and me being forced to leave. I was allowed to go back in one last time. My final words to my father as I held him tightly was "Daddy I love you, and I promise I'll be back first thing in the morning!". He shook his head "no" and looked into my eyes and weakly said "I'm tired, I love you" and tears came out his eyes. He knew that was our goodbye.

I received the call around 11 pm that same night that my father had passed away. Me not being there when he took his last breath was just as painful as the death itself. I felt robbed of not being able to be with him until the end. They took those last moments from me. I went back to the hospital and made arrangements, and when I entered the room to see my father for the last time, it was full of relatives, and I never felt so alone in my entire life. No one there to comfort me.

The sadness continues because not a day goes by that I don't think of him. But God allowed us enough time to make amends with each other, and now my good memories outweigh the bad. Hearing stories from people that knew him best comes quite often. He certainly had an impact on many people including my Halliburton family. He was all of our dads. I'm not sure if the pain of losing a loved one will end and if I could write my father a letter, it'd simply say, "I miss you daddy!" and THAT'S A HELLO!

Love Brown

Love Brown is a TN native, currently residing in Alamo, TN. She is a single mother of two beautiful daughters. Love is a Licensed Practical Nurse at Alamo Nursing and Rehab Center.

"You must read these!"
—Amazon Reviewer

★ ★ ★ ★ ★

TODAY ONLY

Now Available On:
amazon.com

http://www.iamtammylewis.com/